FLORENCE
POCKET GUIDE

Walking Eye
mobile app

Discover the world's best destinations with the Insight Guides Walking Eye app, available to download for free in the App Store and Google Play.

The container app provides easy access to fantastic free content on events and activities taking place in your current location or chosen destination, with the possibility of booking, as well as the regularly-updated Insight Guides travel blog: Inspire Me. In addition, you can purchase curated, premium destination guides through the app, which feature local highlights, hotel, bar, restaurant and shopping listings, an A to Z of practical information and more. Or purchase and download Insight Guides eBooks straight to your device.

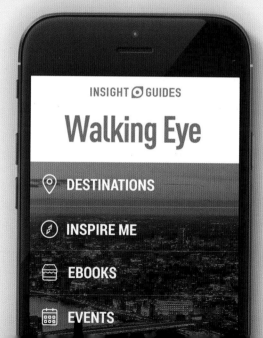

TOP 10 ATTRACTIONS

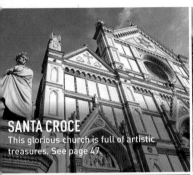

SANTA CROCE
This glorious church is full of artistic treasures. See page 47.

PALAZZO PITTI AND GIARDINO DI BOBOLI
A sumptuous palace and delightful pleasure-garden that once belonged to the Medicis. See pages 69 and 71.

THE DUOMO
Brunelleschi's magnificent dome towers above the city; equally impressive is Giotto's graceful campanile. See page 29.

THE ACCADEMIA
The gallery's star exhibit is Michelangelo's David, perhaps the most famous piece of sculpture in the Western world. See page 61.

PONTE VECCHIO
The beautiful medieval bridge still retains the small shops of its artisans. See page 69.

THE UFFIZI
Home to the world's greatest collection of Italian Renaissance painting. See page 39.

SANTA MARIA NOVELLA
The cavernous church was designed by Dominican architects in the mid-13th century. See page 65.

SAN MARCO
The frescoed dormitory of the monastery is the location of some of Fra Angelico's finest works. See page 60.

SAN LORENZO
The first Renaissance church and home to the glorious Medici Chapels. See page 55.

CAPPELLA BRANCACCI
The site of Masaccio's sublime frescoes. See page 73.

A PERFECT DAY

9.00am

Breakfast
Start your day with a *cappuccino* and *cornetto* at Caffè Scudieri on the Piazza di San Giovanni (19r). This smart, long-established café/*pasticceria* is right in the heart of Florence, in the newly pedestrianised Piazza.

10.00am

The Duomo
Amble around the Piazza, admiring the Baptistery, Campanile (bell tower) and the iconic Duomo (cathedral). Those with stamina can tackle the 463 stairs spiralling to the top of the cathedral's dome to admire Brunelleschi's engineering genius and the fabulous views.

11.30am

Via de'Tornabuoni
Take the Via Roma south of the Baptistery for Piazza della Repubblica, home to some of the city's most elegant cafés. Cross the square for Via Strozzi and at the end turn left into Via de' Tornabuoni for the lavish flagship stores of Armani, Gucci and Prada, to name just a few.

1.00pm

Mercato Nuovo
At Piazza Santa Trinità, turn left into Via Porta, passing halfway along the Palazzo Davanzati. At the end on the right is the Mercato Nuovo; built for the sale of silk and gold, the market is now devoted to leather and souvenirs. Rub the snout of the bronze boar to guarantee your return to Florence and maybe brave a tripe sandwich from the popular stand at the market's southwest corner.

3.00pm

Ponte Vecchio

Head south for the river, passing the famous Uffizi Gallery, repository of the world's finest collection of Renaissance art. At the River Arno turn right for Ponte Vecchio, symbol of Florence and its oldest bridge. Goldsmiths and jewellers have been selling their wares here since 1593.

10.30pm

Nightlife

On summer evenings sit outside and admire the floodlit facade of the Church of Santo Spirito, or join the young Florentines in the lively bars around the piazza.

1.30pm

Piazza art

Since medieval times this expansive piazza has been a hub of city life. Overlooking the piazza is the towering Palazzo Vecchio, former ancestral home of the Medici. Admire the array of open-air sculpture, check out the Gucci Museum, or sit at one of the people-watching cafés. For a juicy *bistecca a la fiorentin*a and a glass of Chianti, head for nearby Frescobaldi (Via dei Magazzini).

3.30pm

Boboli

From the bridge follow the flow to the Palazzo Pitti. The vast palace is home to five museums and could occupy a whole day or more. For now just explore the lovely Giardino di Boboli, the formal gardens dotted with loggias, cool fountains, grottos and myriad statues.

8.00pm

Dinner time

Make for Piazza Santo Spirito, just northwest of Palazzo Pitti. Relax with an *aperitivo* on the piazza and then choose a spot for dinner. The piazza buzzes with cafés, restaurants and wine bars.

CONTENTS

INTRODUCTION

The magnificent view from the hilltop church of San Miniato has changed little since the 16th century, where the belvedere looks out across the bridge-trellised Arno to Florence's *centro storico* (historic centre). It is a sea of terracotta rooftops interrupted only by the cupola (dome) of San Lorenzo, the medieval bell-tower of the Palazzo Vecchio and the focal point; the massive cupola of the Duomo.

The massive contribution that Florence made to Western civilisation and culture was greatly out of proportion to its then diminutive size. Few nations, let alone cities, can boast of having nurtured such a remarkable heritage of artistic, literary, scientific and political talent in such a short period of time. Florence was, as D.H. Lawrence put it, 'man's perfect universe'.

Travel guides often compare Renaissance Florence with Athens in the 5th century BC, but while that glory is recalled only by spectacular ruins, Renaissance Florence remains is alive and well. Its historic palaces, great churches, exquisite sculptures and countless masterpieces are not crumbling relics, but a vivid and functional part of everyday life – worked in, lived in, prayed in, prized, and open to all.

The elegant Palazzo Vecchio, where the first civic authority sat in the Middle Ages, still houses the offices of the city council. Congregations kneel for mass in churches commissioned by medieval guilds. The jewellery stores lining the Ponte Vecchio are occupied by the descendants of goldsmiths who set up workshops here in the 14th century. Most of the city's narrow, cobbled side streets

Famous sons

Some of the greatest names in European culture – Dante, Boccaccio, Giotto, Donatello, Botticelli, Michelangelo, Leonardo, Cellini and Machiavelli – lived and worked in Florence.

Capturing the city's stunning skyline

were wide enough to permit the passage of horse-drawn carts of centuries ago.

Not surprisingly, the city has proved irresistible to tourists since the late 18th century, when Florence and its treasures became an unmissable stop on the 'Grand Tour' undertaken by the British gentry. Today, the medieval alleys are lined with ice cream bars, souvenir shops and pizzerias. Yet among the trappings of modern tourism, the bronze-workers and leather artisans can still be found in their workshops.

Florence's detractors describe the city as overcrowded and overpriced. There is a modicum of truth in such criticism, but the crowds, and to a certain extent the high prices, can be avoided by visiting in low season. You will never escape the overwhelming impact of so much superlative art and architecture, even if you have only a few days to see it. Be selective, pick out a few highlights and absorb them at your leisure. If you try to cover everything you will end up exhausted and remembering little.

TRIALS AND TRIBULATIONS

The medieval Florentines were considered pragmatic, hard working, inventive and sharp witted. These qualities are evident in today's inhabitants, along with an innate sense of dignity, elegance and a savage pride in their city and its patrimony.

The Florentines' resilience has been illustrated throughout history, and never more clearly than during the disastrous flood of November 1966. Swollen by heavy rains, the Arno burst its banks one night. In certain parts of the city the water reached depths of 7m (23ft) – small plaques around town indicate the height of the flood. Thick mud, mixed with damaging oil from ruptured tanks, swirled into shops and museums.

Countless paintings, frescoes, sculptures and antique books were severely damaged. Florentines joined in the Herculean task of rescuing what they could and helping to clear debris and repair the urban fabric. Restoring damaged works of art was entrusted to an international team of experts, some of whom are still working today. Most of the affected works of

THE MEDICI ARMS

Students of heraldry will be busy in Florence, for the coats of arms of wealthy families, trade guilds and sponsors embellish the facades of many palaces, towers and churches.

The most famous are the ubiquitous arms of the Medici family, with their six balls. There has been much speculation on their meaning, but some say that the balls represent pills, for the Medici, whose name means 'doctors', were originally members of the guild of spice merchants and apothecaries; they later made their fame and fortune in textiles and banking. Five balls are coloured red, but the top ball is blue and bears the golden lily of France – a gift from Louis XI of France in the 15th century.

art are now back on display in Florence's galleries.

The people's resolve was tested once again in May 1993, when a Mafia car bomb tore apart the west wing of the Uffizi Gallery, killing five people. Irreparable damage to the collection was limited thanks to protective plexiglass shields. Two hundred works were damaged, 37 of them seriously, and remarkably only two beyond repair. Twenty odd years on, the Uffizi is undergoing a long-overdue

Evidence of the city's artistic heritage is abundant

redevelopment, with major changes. The multimillion-euro 'Nuovi Uffizi' (New Uffizi) will ease access problems, double the exhibition space and give visitors the chance to see many works that were previously archived. Two new suites of rooms opened in 2011 and 2012, adding another 19 rooms.

It is perhaps this sense of being custodians of the legacy of the Renaissance, and heirs to an unmatched tradition of excellence, that gives the Florentines an almost Medici-like pride in their city. This feeling of continuity with the past is what makes Florence such a uniquely evocative place. Its unparalleled masterworks are viewed as a living record of an extraordinary period of innovation.

For this reason alone, Florence deserves all the superlatives that are shamelessly showered upon it. What's more, if the heat, crowds and queues become too much, escape to a hilltop across the river, and savour the same view that Michelangelo savoured.

A BRIEF HISTORY

No one quite knows how the Roman town of Florentia came by its name. According to some, it was named after Florinus, a Roman general who in 63 BC encamped on the city's future site to besiege the nearby hill town of Fiesole, ruled by the Etruscans, Italy's pre-Roman lords. Others maintain that the name refers to the abundance of flowers in the region, or perhaps even to the 'flourishing' of the successful riverside town.

Whatever the origin of its name, Roman Florence had developed into a thriving military and commercial settlement by around 59 BC. If you take a walk along the aptly named Via Romana on the south bank of the Arno and cross the Ponte Vecchio towards the city centre, you'll be following in the steps of the Roman legions, travellers and merchants of 2,000 years ago. Even though you will find no visible Roman remains in Florence itself, all the trappings of civilised Roman life were once located here, including a forum, baths, temples and a theatre. You can see more of this era in neighbouring Fiesole, which has a number of Etruscan and Roman ruins dating to the 1st century BC.

A clay sarcophagus cover, portraying Larthia Seianti from Chiusi

FROM THE CAROLINGIANS TO THE REPUBLIC

A few centuries later, invasions from the north and the fall of the Western Roman Empire (AD 476) plunged Europe into a turbulent period of history. This was briefly relieved by the sway of the Frankish king, Charlemagne, and his vast European empire of the 8th and 9th centuries. However, by the 10th century even greater chaos had set in.

Somehow the Carolingian province of Tuscany survived. In the late 11th century, Florence made rapid commercial and political progress under a remarkable ruler, Mathilda, the Grand Countess of Tuscany. The great guilds (arti maggiori) came into being in this period. These influential bodies might be seen as the precursors of today's trade

Matilda of Tuscany, c.1111

unions, set up to protect the interests of the apothecaries and the wool, silk and spice merchants, among others. By 1138, just 23 years after Mathilda's death, Florence had developed into a self-governing republic and a power to be reckoned with.

At that time, Florence presented an appearance very different from that of today's city. The wealthy merchant families fortified their homes with square stone towers, often more than 70m (230ft) high, to serve as impregnable refuges during the recurring feuds that split the community. By the end of the 12th century, the city's skyline bristled with over 150 towers. Only a few have survived, but a better idea of the town's early appearance can be grasped in the Tuscan hill town of San Gimignano (see page 84).

GUELPHS AND GHIBELLINES

Eventually the interests of an aristocratic elite and a rising merchant class were bound to clash. When they did, Florence's development declined into a series of savage factional struggles. The nobility opposed the broader-based forms of government that the merchants promoted and the situation was aggravated by fierce inter-family feuds and continual raids on Florentine trade by 'robber barons'.

San Miniato's facade dates from the 11th century

To make matters worse, powerful foreign interests became involved. The pro-Pope Guelph and pro-Emperor Ghibelline parties (see box), which first developed in the 13th century, had their origins in other Italian cities where the ambitions of the Papacy and the Holy Roman Empire (founded in AD 962) were dangerously divergent. Other Tuscan cities soon followed suit with their own Guelph-Ghibelline factions, and Tuscany remained in a state of turmoil for more than two centuries. Pisa, Lucca, Pistoia, Siena, Arezzo and Florence became in turn enemies or allies, depending on which party held power in which town.

EVOLUTION OF FLORENTINE SOCIETY

In spite of these setbacks, Florentine commerce and banking continued to develop, and its woollen-cloth trade prospered.

The first gold *fiorino* was minted in the mid-13th century. With the city's patron St Giovanni on one side and the symbolic Florentine lily on the other, it was rapidly adopted throughout Europe as the standard unit of currency.

The city's social evolution during this time was remarkable. Organised 'factories' or workshops were opened. Hospitals, schools and charitable societies were founded. The university, one of Europe's oldest, turned out lawyers, teachers and doctors. Streets were paved, laws were passed regulating noise and nuisance, and the Brotherhood of the Misericordia, a forerunner of the Red Cross, was established (see page 33). Although life was hard and Florence was never a democracy in the modern sense of the word, the city gave its citizens a unique feeling of belonging that overcame class or party differences.

In spite of their internal divisions, the Guelphs gradually edged the Ghibellines out of power. By the late 13th century, the bankers, merchants and city guilds had a firm grasp on the helm of the Florentine republic and felt secure enough to turn their attention to the building of a fitting seat of government. Already involved with the construction of a sumptuous cathedral, a mighty palace of the people – the Palazzo del Popolo – was begun in 1298. This was later renamed the Palazzo della Signoria and is now known as the Palazzo Vecchio. Located in the Piazza della Signoria, it still serves as the city hall, after having followed a brief stint as a Medici residence during the Renaissance. The palazzo is one of the most handsome surviving structures from this period.

Pope vs Emperor

The names 'Guelph' (supporters of the Pope) and 'Ghibelline' (supporters of the Holy Roman Emperor) are said to come from the German Welf (dukes of Bavaria) and Waiblingen (the home of the Hohenstaufens) respectively.

FLORENCE'S GOLDEN AGE

Florentine bankers now held the purse strings of Europe, with agents in every major city. One group, headed by the Bardi and Peruzzi families, lent Edward III of England 1,365,000 gold florins to finance his campaigns against the French. Then in 1343 the double-dealing Edward suddenly declared himself bankrupt, and toppled the entire banking system.

As always, the resilient Florentines recovered, and the merchant interests set out with ruthless zeal to regain their lost prestige. Despite ceaseless social unrest, violent riots, disastrous floods, and the Black Death of 1347–8, which claimed over half the city's population (and one-third of Italy's), by the early 1400s Florence found itself stronger and richer than ever. The foundation had been laid for its brightest moment to come.

In addition to commercial success, the city's cultural life was flourishing, moving towards the early years of what was to become known as the Renaissance. Interest was reviving in long-neglected Greek and Latin literature. While Florentine historians started recording their city's progress for posterity, merchant guilds and the nouveaux riches found time between business deals and party vendettas to indulge in artistic patronage.

Despite factional divisions, the Florentines were able to plan ambitious public works and awe-inspiring private palazzos. The Duomo, Giotto's Campanile, the great monastic churches of Santa Croce and Santa Maria Novella, the Bargello and the Palazzo Vecchio were all begun or completed during the tumultuous 14th century.

The power of the important business families, the *signori*, was slowly proving to be greater than that of the guilds. The ambitious Medici, a family of wealthy wool merchants and bankers, came to dominate every facet of Florentine life for

60 golden years (1434–94) and, to a diminishing degree, the decades thereafter. The Medici were shrewd politicians and enthusiastic and discerning patrons of the arts. As patrons they led the city and its people to unparalleled heights of civilisation, at a time when most of Europe was struggling to free itself from the coarse, tangled mesh of medieval feudalism.

THE RENAISSANCE

The term 'Renaissance' *(Rinascimento)* was coined by 16th-century Florentine artist and historian Giorgio Vasari (1511–74), whose book *Lives of the Most Excellent Painters, Sculptors and Architects* tells almost everything we know about the great Italian artists from the 13th century up to his own time. 'Renaissance' means 'rebirth', which is exactly how Vasari saw the events of the 15th century: The world appeared to be waking from a long sleep and taking up life where antiquity had

Artisans at work, depicted on the church of Orsanmichele

Resurrection of the Son of Theophilus by Filippino Lippi

left off. The Church had dominated the cultural life of Europe throughout the Middle Ages. Literature, architecture, painting, sculpture and music were all aimed at the glorification of God, rather than the celebration of earthly life and beauty. The Greek and Roman concept of 'art for art's sake' had been forgotten until it was revived in 15th-century Florence; a comparison of Cimabue's *Virgin Enthroned* (c.1290) with *La Primavera* by Botticelli (1477–8) illustrates the difference between the art of the Middle Ages and the Renaissance.

The idea had taken hold that life must be lived to its fullest and that the pursuit of earthly knowledge, beauty and pleasure were what counted most in the brief time allotted to man. The arts and sciences of the Renaissance were directed towards those ends.

THE MEDICI

Although few of the early Medici ever held office in city government, three of them were in fact the true rulers of

Florence. They were: Cosimo, *Il Vecchio* ('the Elder', 1389–1464), a munificent patron of the arts and letters and founder of the Medici dynasty, who earned himself the title *pater-patriae* ('father of his country'); his son, Piero, *Il Gottoso* ('the Gouty', 1416–69); and his grandson Lorenzo, *Il Magnifico* ('the Magnificent', 1449–92). Ably pulling strings via supporters elected to the republican government (the *Signoria*), all three were expert politicians who knew how to win the hearts and minds of the Florentine masses.

Lorenzo's diplomatic skill kept Italy temporarily free of wars and invasions, and his love of the arts had a direct effect on cultural life as we know it today. On Lorenzo's death in 1492, his son Piero, lo Sfortunato ('the Unfortunate'), took his place. Loutish and devoid of taste, Piero was deemed unworthy of the Medici name and lasted just two years. When Charles VIII of France invaded Italy, Piero first opposed him but suddenly changed sides as it became clear that the French were winning. He had to accept humiliating terms of settlement. The Florentine people were so enraged that they drove him from the city and set up a republic. It was at this time that Niccolò Machiavelli held office in Florence, gaining first-hand experience in the arts of intrigue and diplomacy.

BONFIRE OF THE VANITIES

The spiritual force behind the new republic was a fanatical Dominican friar from Ferrara, Girolamo Savonarola (1452–98). Prior of the Monastery of San Marco, he preached regularly in the Duomo during Lorenzo's last years. At first the Florentines ignored

Lorenzo de' Medici

Poet, naturalist, art collector, dabbler in philosophy and architecture, Lorenzo was perhaps the most outstanding member of the Medici dynasty. He was an example of what is still referred to as a 'Renaissance man'.

Lorenzo de' Medici

his message of the decadence of the Renaissance. However, by 1490 thousands had heard him inveigh against the excesses of the Medici courts, prophesying apocalyptic punishments for the city if its people did not embrace a more godly way of life.

In 1494, he decreed the destruction of the 'vanities' of art, and Florentines flocked to the Piazza della Signoria with armfuls of illuminated books, hand-loomed textiles and precious paintings, which they hurled upon a huge bonfire in the middle of the square. Even Botticelli joined in, flinging some of his own paintings into the flames. But Savonarola had powerful enemies (Pope Borgia, for one) who soon brought about his downfall. He was arrested, sentenced to death for heresy, and hanged and burned where his 'bonfire of the vanities' had taken place four years earlier. A bronze plaque still marks the spot in Piazza della Signoria.

In 1512, Piero's brothers, Giovanni and Giuliano, returned to Florence, putting an end to the republic. Expelled in 1527, the persistent Medici were back three years later, after an eight-month siege, with the help of the Holy Roman Emperor Charles V.

During the subsequent rule of Grand Duke Cosimo I de' Medici (1537–1574), an attempt was made to revive the spirit of the Medici's earlier golden age. Some of Florence's most prominent monuments date from this period, including the Santa Trinità Bridge, the Boboli Garden (Cosimo's back garden when residing in the Palazzo Pitti), the Neptune Fountain in the Piazza della Signoria, and Cellini's magnificent bronze *Perseus*, a copy of which stands in the Loggia dei Lanzi in Piazza della Signoria.

THE 18TH AND 19TH CENTURIES

Under the rule of the grand dukes of Tuscany (Medici until 1737, then Hapsburgs up to 1859), Florence sank into a torpor that lasted for more than three centuries. Anna Maria Ludovica, last of the Medici line, who died in 1749, made a grand final gesture worthy of her Renaissance forebears. With foresight she bequeathed the entire Medici art collection to the city 'to attract foreigners', on condition that none of it ever be sold or removed from Florence. This became the basis of the staggering collection of the Uffizi Gallery, formerly the offices of the Medici.

Her wish was granted, for the foreigners came, at first in a small but steady trickle of privileged young gentlemen on

FLORENTINE EXPLORERS

Amerigo Vespucci (1454–1512) went down in history as the man who gave his name to America. Banker, businessman and navigator, he crossed the Atlantic in the wake of Christopher Columbus (who was from Genoa), and explored the coast of South America, discovering the estuaries of the Orinoco and Rio de la Plata. His main achievement was to ascertain that Columbus had, in fact, discovered a 'New World', and not Asia, as Columbus himself had maintained.

More than 20 years later, another Florentine navigator, Giovanni da Verrazzano (1485–1528), searching for the legendary Northwest Passage, sailed through the narrows that now bear his name, and discovered New York Harbour.

Opposing views

Visitors' opinions about the city have varied widely. Shelley called Florence a 'paradise of exiles', Walter Savage Landor 'the filthiest capital in Europe' and Aldous Huxley 'a second-rate provincial town with... repulsive Gothic architecture'.

the Grand Tour of Europe. However, in the early 19th century a new breed of traveller appeared, the 'Italianate Englishman', led by the poets Byron and Shelley. Later in the century the Brownings, John Ruskin (although his major work was on Venice), and the Ruskin-inspired Pre-Raphaelites followed. Rapturous Britons, who were smitten by the mythologised and romantic image of Italy, toured or settled in droves, bringing in their wake French, German and Russian tourists, all referred to as 'the English' by the Florentines. Queen Victoria herself visited the city. Florence Nightingale was named after the city of her birth (there is a statue of her in the Santa Croce cloister); she would go on to make her mark in the Crimean War.

After the dramatic events of the Risorgimento, when the occupying Austrians were expelled, Florence had a brief moment of glory as the capital of the newly unified kingdom of Italy (1865–71). With the later transfer of the capital to Rome, the story of Florence merged into Italian history.

EARLY 20TH CENTURY

Despite the excitement at the time of unification, the early years of independence were turbulent. Political crisis followed crisis, and governments became vulnerable to attack from reactionary forces. During World War I, Italy fought against Germany and Austria, but afterwards the feeling that it had been insufficiently rewarded for its sacrifices was exploited by the fascist Benito Mussolini, who seized power in 1922 and declared himself prime minister of Italy.

WORLD WAR II TO THE PRESENT DAY

With the Rome–Berlin Axis of 1937, Mussolini linked the fate of Italy to Hitler's Germany, dragging his country to defeat in World War II. The fascist government fell in 1943, with some of the most heroic battles of the Italian resistance fought in and around Florence. The retreating Germans blew up all the bridges over the Arno except for the Ponte Vecchio, spared, it is believed, because of its famous past. The city's art treasures and landmark architecture survived unscathed. Mussolini and his mistress came to a sticky end. They were executed in 1945 and their bodies displayed in Milan.

Since 1945 the city has continued to see destruction on a large scale. On 4 November 1966 the Arno broke its banks, causing immense damage to many of the city's artworks and killing 35 people. In 1993 a Mafia bomb exploded by the Uffizi,

German paratroopers face Allied soldiers across the Arno

Dario Nardella, Florence's current mayor

killing five people and damaging around 200 precious works of art.

Today, Florence is a lively university city and a major tourist destination with nearly 8 million visitors a year. The preservation of its remarkable cultural heritage has given rise not only to economic pressures but controversy over much-needed infrastructure projects. Debates still rage over the proposed avant-garde exit to the Uffizi Gallery, the Tramvia (new tram system) and Norman Foster's new underground railway station.

Since 2009, Florence has had a succession of progressive young mayors. Matteo Renzi, of the Democratic Party, was the city's mayor from 2009–2014. During his time in office, Renzi reinvigorated the city's political and cultural scene, invested in eco-friendly transport and pressed for the preservation of the city's green spaces. Almost as soon as he was elected, Renzi announced that the Piazza Duomo, in the heart of the city, would become a pedestrian only zone, and banned all traffic. Following Renzi's election as Prime Minister of Italy in 2014, Dario Nardella, another young and energetic politician from the Democratic Party became Florence's mayor. So far, Nardella has overseen the continued expansion and reconstruction of the Uffizi; the reopening of Museo dell'Opera del in 2015 following a major restoration; and in 2016, the oldest theatre in Florence, the Teatro Niccolini, reopened after a 20-year closure.

HISTORICAL LANDMARKS

8th century BC The first settlements on the site of Florence.

c.59BC The foundation of the Roman city of Florentia.

3rd century AD St Minias brings Christianity to Florence.

570 The Lombards take control of Tuscany.

774 Charlemagne defeats the Lombards and takes over Tuscany.

1115 Florence becomes a self-governing commune.

1215 Beginning of the conflict between the Guelphs and Ghibellines.

1296–9 Work begins on the Duomo and Palazzo Vecchio.

1302 Dante expelled in a mass purge of the Ghibellines.

1347–8 The Black Death kills over half of the city's population.

1400 onwards The beginning of the Renaissance and the rise of Florence as the pre-eminent cultural centre in Europe.

1434–64 Cosimo de' Medici rules Florence.

1469–92 The rule of Lorenzo 'the Magnificent'.

1494–8 Florence becomes a republic under the rule of Christ.

1512 The Medici regain control of the city.

1537–74 The rule of Cosimo I; Florence goes into slow decline.

1610 Galileo made court mathematician to Cosimo II.

1737 The death of Gian Gastone, last Medici ruler of Florence.

1860 Tuscany becomes part of emerging United Kingdom of Italy.

1865–71 Florence is capital of the new kingdom.

1944 The retreating Germans destroy three bridges of the Arno.

1966 Florence is devastated by floods.

1993 A Mafia bomb kills five people and damages the Uffizi.

2002 The euro replaces the Italian lira as the main unit of currency.

2010 Opening of Line 1 of Florence's long-awaited Tramvia.

2011–12 19 new rooms open in the Uffizi Gallery.

2014 Florence's former mayor, Matteo Renzi, becomes the Prime Minster of Italy. Dario Nardella replaces him as Mayor of Florence.

2015 Florence hosts many events related to the EXPO 2015 – the world's largest exhibition on nutrition– which was based in Milan.

2016 Florence's oldest theatre, the Teatro Niccolini, reopens after a 20-year closure.

WHERE TO GO

Although Florence's suburbs spread far along the Arno Valley, the old part of the city is compact and easy to negotiate on foot, with most of the sights of interest to visitors. On the northern bank of the River Arno is the *centro storico* (historic centre), laid out around three large squares. Around the edge of the *centro storico* are three of the city's most important churches, San Lorenzo, San Marco and Santa Maria Novella. Across the river is the district of Oltrarno. Settled later than the north bank, this was once an area of workshops and artisans and still retains a more laid-back air than the heavily touristed streets around the Duomo and Piazza della Signoria.

PIAZZA DEL DUOMO

The superb **Piazza del Duomo** is situated to the north of the grid of narrow streets that make up Florence's *centro storico*. At its centre, the magnificent cathedral is the symbolic heart of the city and remains its tallest building.

THE DUOMO

The huge multicoloured facade of the **Duomo ❶** (www.museum florence.com; Mon–Wed, Fri 10am–5pm, Thu 10am–4.30pm, Sat 10am–4.45pm, Sun 1.30–4.45pm; free) rises majestically alongside the pointed roof of the Baptistery.

Officially known as Santa Maria dei Fiori (Saint Mary of the Flowers), the Duomo was designed by the great architect Arnolfo di Cambio (1245–1302), who was also responsible for the Palazzo Vecchio (see page 35). This new cathedral was intended to surpass all of the great buildings of antiquity in both size and splendour.

Work commenced around 1296 on the site of the far smaller

Santa Maria del Fiore, in Piazza del Duomo

5th-century cathedral of Santa Reparata, but was not completed until the second half of the 15th century. The cathedral's wonderfully elaborate, neo-Gothic facade was added as late as the 19th century. Like the majority of Tuscan churches of the time, the Duomo presents a unique local version of Gothic architecture that is not easily compared to other northern European ecclesiastical buildings of the same period.

The mighty **cupola** was the contribution of Filippo Brunelleschi (1377–1446), the first true 'Renaissance' architect, who was inspired by the dome on Rome's Pantheon, rebuilt for Emperor Hadrian in about AD 125.

When the ambitious Florentines decided that their showpiece cathedral must have a great dome, they held a public competition in 1418. Brunelleschi submitted the winning design (encouraged by the organisers to make *it il più bello che si può* 'as beautiful as possible') and, just as important,

The cathedral is Florence's tallest building at 107m (351ft)

architecturally sound. His original wooden model can be seen in the Museo dell'Opera del Duomo (see page 34). In Florence, where beauty and art were never the preserve of the rich alone, these competitions used to cause immense, popular excitement.

Brunelleschi's magnificent dome, the first giant cupola since antiquity, was completed in 1436. It was visible for miles, dwarfing the red-tiled rooftops around it, and confirming the feeling of the day that nothing was beyond the science and ingenuity of man.

A long climb

You can climb up the spiralling 463 steps to the lantern at its top and enjoy breathtaking panoramic views over the city. Entry to the steps is via the Porta della Mandoria (Mon–Fri 8.30am–6.20pm, Sat 8.30am–5pm, Sun 1–4pm; combined ticket) on the northern side of the Duomo.

By contrast with the polychrome exterior, the cathedral's **interior** is strikingly vast and stark. Although most of the original statuary was long ago moved to the Museo dell'Opera del Duomo, there are still some important works of art to be seen, such as the magnificent 16th-century fresco on the inside of the cupola. The depiction of *The Last Judgement* was begun by Giorgio Vasari and finished by his student Federico Zuccari.

Lorenzo Ghiberti's bronze shrine below the high altar was made to house the remains of St Zenobius, one of Florence's first bishops.

Left of the entrance are some unusual *trompe l'œil* frescoes of two 15th-century *condottieri* (mercenary captains) who fought for Florence. The right-hand one, painted by the great master of perspective Paolo Uccello, commemorates an Englishman, John Hawkwood. He was the only foreigner ever buried in the Duomo, although his remains were later repatriated. Uccello is also responsible for the 1443 **ora italica** clock next to Ghiberti's windows.

On the right, just inside the cathedral's entrance, are the steps down to the **crypt** (closed Sun, last entry 30 mins before closing), which contains Brunelleschi's simple tomb.

THE CAMPANILE

The Duomo's free-standing **Campanile di Giotto ❷** (www. museumflorence.com; daily 8.15am–6.50pm; combined ticket) is one of Florence's most graceful landmarks. The bell-tower was begun in 1334 by Giotto, and completed in 1359 by his successors Andrea Pisano and Andrea Talenti. Faced in green, white and pink marble to match the Duomo, the lowest storey bears hexagonal reliefs illustrating *Genesis* and various arts and industries by Pisano and Luca della Robbia. The niches in the second storey contain statues of the Prophets and Sibyls, some by Donatello. It is worth making the 414-step climb to the top for a bird's-eye view of the cathedral and a city that was never permitted to build higher than the cathedral's dome.

THE BAPTISTERY

Opposite the Duomo lies **Il Battistero ❸** (www.museum florence.com; Mon–Wed and Fri 8.15–10.15am and 11.15am–6.30pm, Thu–Sat 8.15am–6.30pm, Sun 8.15am–1.30pm; combined ticket). Acclaimed as Florence's oldest building, this precious gem of octagonal Romanesque architecture, served for a time as the city's cathedral. It was built in the early part of the 12th century on what is believed to be the site of a Roman temple. With the exception of its doors, the exterior appearance remains as it was in the time of Dante. Brilliant 13th-century mosaics inside the cupola include scenes from the *Creation*, *Life of St John* and an 8m (26ft) figure of Christ in the *Last Judgement*.

The Baptistery's principal claim to fame is its three sets of **gilded bronze doors** (originals in the Museo dell'Opera del Duomo). Those on the south side are the oldest. Dating from the 14th century, they are the work of Andrea Pisano. A competition to design another set of doors was held in 1401, financed by one of the merchant guilds. Brunelleschi was among those who submitted an entry, but Lorenzo Ghiberti's submission was declared the winner. Their original entries are now in the Bargello. The first doors Ghiberti produced can be seen on the north side of the Baptistery. The artist later went on to make the magnificent east doors, facing the Duomo and therefore the most important, which were described by an admir-

Part of Ghiberti's gilded 'Gates of Paradise'

ing Michelangelo as being fit to be the 'Gates of Paradise'. The name has stuck ever since.

LOGGIA DEL BIGALLO

On the corner of Via dei Calzaiuoli, south of the Baptistery, is the graceful 14th-century **Loggia del Bigallo**. The loggia (covered gallery) was once part of the headquarters of the **Brotherhood of the Misericordia**, a society for the care of orphans and one of Florence's oldest and most respected social institutions. It is now a small museum (tel: 055-288 496; reservations required) with some fine works of art and a tourist point. Across the street from the loggia lie the brotherhood's current headquarters. Founded by St Peter Martyr in 1244, the society was especially needed during frequent bouts of pestilence and plague. Today's unpaid volunteers, easily recognised in their black hooded capes, provide free assistance to the poor and needy, and also run an ambulance service.

MUSEO DELL'OPERA DEL DUOMO

At the east end of the piazza, the **Museo dell'Opera del Duomo** ❹ (www.museumflorence.com; daily 9am–7pm; combined ticket), expanded and beautifully restored in 2015, holds many of the Duomo's most precious treasures and original sculptures in its 25 rooms, which are spread over three floors. After 27 years of restoration, the original bronze panels of Ghiberti's Gates of Paradise, designed for the Baptistery, were finally put together. The gates are on display at the Salone del Paradiso; the grandest hall of the revamped museum. The sumptuous 14th–15th-century silver-faced altar is also from the Baptistery. Other treasures include rich gold and silver reliquaries, one of which supposedly houses the index finger of St John, Florence's patron saint. Brunelleschi's original wooden model of the Duomo's cupola is also here, as is Donatello's harrowing wooden effigy of Mary Magdalene and the *Zuccone* that once graced the Campanile. The two beautiful sculptured choir lofts (*cantorie*) are by Donatello and Luca della Robbia respectively. The museum also houses Michelangelo's unfinished *Pietà*, which may have been intended for his own tomb.

PIAZZA DELLA SIGNORIA

The second major square of the *centro storico* is **Piazza della Signoria** ❺. If the Piazza del Duomo is the religious heart of Florence, this piazza is its political and social counterpart. The city rulers have gathered here since the 13th century, and the present-day offices of the city council are still housed in the austere Palazzo Vecchio.

PALAZZO VECCHIO

Dominating the square is the fortress-like **Palazzo Vecchio** ⑥ (www.museicivicifiorentini.it; Apr–Sept Mon–Wed and Fri–Sun 9am–midnight, Thu 9am–2pm, Oct–Mar Mon–Wed Fri–Sun 9am–7pm, Thu 9am–2pm), also known as the Palazzo della Signoria after the highest tier of the city's 15th-century government, the *Signoria*, which convened here. Designed in 1299 by Arnolfo di Cambio, who also designed the Duomo, it was intended to house the city's government. After serving briefly as a Medici residence, it acquired the name Palazzo Vecchio (Old Palace) in 1550 when the Medici moved their headquarters over the river to the new Palazzo Pitti (see page 69).

The palazzo's off-centre 94m (308ft) tower, added in 1310, helps to soften the building's squareness and comple-ments its off-centre position on the piazza.

The imposing Palazzo Vecchio

The palazzo's interior comes as a surprise after the medieval austerity of the exterior. It was completely remodelled when Cosimo I de' Medici moved in, in 1540. The **courtyard,** designed by Michelozzi Michelozzo in 1453, is delightful. Vasari, who also designed the foun-tain at the centre, added the ornate stucco and frescoes in 1565. Verrocchio's bronze fountainhead depicting a putto with a dolphin was

The palazzo's inner courtyard, designed by Michelozzo in 1453

brought here from Lorenzo de' Medici's villa at Careggi. What you see here is a copy; the original is displayed upstairs.

The palazzo's highlights include the massive **Salone dei Cinquecento**, on the first floor. Built to house the parliament of the short-lived Florentine republic declared in 1494, Cosimo I later turned it into a grand throne room. He had it decorated with giant Vasari frescoes of Florentine victories and Michelangelo's statue *The Genius of Victory*, representing Cosimo's triumph over enemy Siena in 1554–5. Three centuries later, the first parliament of a united Italy met here. It is still used today for special government functions.

A small door to the right of the main entrance leads into the **Studiolo di Francesco I** (only accessible on a guided tour), a little gem of a study designed by Vasari. It is covered from floor to barrel-vaulted ceiling with painted allegorical panels (representing *Fire*, *Water*, *Earth* and *Air*), and two Bronzino portraits of Cosimo I and his consort gazing down haughtily.

Across the hall, another door leads into the **Quartiere di Leone X**, the apartments of the first Medici pope. The rooms are sumptuously decorated with frescoes celebrating the achievements of the Medici family. Stairs lead up to the equally sumptuous **Quartiere degli Elementi**, with painted allegories on the theme of the elements. The Terraza di Saturno at the back provides a fine view across the river.

A gallery above the Salone dei Cinquecento leads to the **Quartiere di Eleonora** (the apartments of Cosimo I's Spanish wife), a riot of gilt, painted ceilings and rich furnishings.

The splendid 15th-century **Sala dei Gigli** (Hall of the Lilies), all blue and gold, is lavishly decorated with Florentine heraldry, a gilt-panelled ceiling, bright Ghirlandaio frescoes, and superb doors inlaid with figures of Dante and Petrarch. Here stands Donatello's original bronze of *Judith and Holofernes*. A copy is in the piazza outside.

Next door is the splendid **Sala Mappamondo,** a cupboard-lined room whose wooden panels were painted with maps by two learned Dominican friars (1563–87). In 2012 the soaring Tower of Palazzo Vecchio (Apr–Sept Mon–Wed, Fri–Sun 9am–8.30pm, Thu 9am–2pm, Oct–Mar Mon–Wed, Fri–Sun 10am–5pm, Thu 10am–2pm), affording fine views, was opened to the public for the first time.

LOGGIA DEI LANZI

On the south side of the Piazza della Signoria is the Loggia della Signoria, more commonly known as the **Loggia dei Lanzi**, built in the late 14th century. Originally a covered vantage point for city officials at public ceremonies, it took its later name from Cosimo I's Swiss-German mercenary bodyguards, known as *Landsknechts* (Italianised to *Lanzichenecchi*), who used it as a guardroom during his nine-year residence in the Palazzo Vecchio. Since the late 18th century the loggia has officially been an open-air sculpture museum, but celebrated works of art have been displayed here since long before then. Cellini's fine bronze *Perseus* was originally placed here, on Cosimo's order in 1554. Giambologna's famous *Rape of the Sabine Women* was added in 1583, while his *Hercules and the Centaur* and the Roman statues at the back, donated by the Medici, were added towards the end of the 18th century.

In front of the palazzo a *marzocco* – a heraldic lion bearing the city's arms (the symbol of Florence) – has graced the piazza for almost as long as the palazzo itself. What you see today is a copy; the original is in the Bargello. Michelangelo's *David* was positioned here in 1504 as a republican symbol, but was moved to the Accademia (see page 61) in 1873 and replaced with a copy. The present version is an early 20th-century copy; a bronze version can be found across the river in the Piazzale Michelangelo. The rather grotesque statue of *Hercules and Cacus*, beside *David*, is the work of a 16th-century sculptor, Bandinelli.

Giambologna's Rape of the Sabine Women

THE GUCCI MUSEO

The Gucci Museo (www.gucci museo.com; Piazza Signoria, Sun–Thu and Sat 10am–8pm, Fri 10am–11pm; café and restaurant, Sun–Thu 10am–8pm, Fri–Sat 10am–11pm), opened in 2012, provides light relief from Renaissance sculpture. Gucci exhibits (think zebra skin suitcases, Oscar gowns and monogrammed flippers) are juxtaposed with contemporary art installations from the collection of French retail magnate François Pinault.

THE UFFIZI

Between the Palazzo Vecchio and the Arno, the **Galleria degli Uffizi ❼** (Uffizi Gallery; www.uffizi.com; Tue–Sun 8.15am–6.50pm) stretches down either side of the narrow Piazzale degli Uffizi. This was Vasari's greatest architectural work. Built in the second half of the 16th century, the building was intended to house the headquarters of various government offices (*uffizi* is Old Italian for 'offices'), the official mint and workshops for Medici craftsmen. It is now the home of one of the world's most famous and important art galleries.

There are usually long queues to get in, and the gallery can be very crowded. To avoid the queues, book a timed entrance ticket in advance online at www.uffizi.com or by contacting Firenze Musei (tel: 055-294 883; www.firenzemusei.it), although it costs a little more. The Firenze Card also enables you to skip the queues.

The Uffizi has been undergoing a massive and painfully slow redevelopment since 1989, and the work is far from complete. The Nuovi Uffizi project (www.nuoviuffizi.it) will double the number of paintings on show and allow twice as many visitors to the gallery. Some ideas, however, have not been without controversy, especially the avant-garde design for a new exit by the Japanese architect Arata Isozaki, which has been at a standstill since 2003. During renovations many works of art have been rearranged or moved to different galleries.

Exhibited in chronological order, the paintings comprise the cream of Italian and European art from the 13th to 18th centuries. Begun by Cosimo I and added to by his successors, the collection was bequeathed to the people of Florence in perpetuity in 1737 by Anna Maria Ludovica, the last of the Medici dynasty, on condition that it never leave the city.

The first rooms contain those early Tuscan greats, **Cimabue** and **Giotto**. In their altarpieces depicting enthroned Madonnas (painted in 1280 and 1310, respectively), the mosaic-like stiffness of Cimabue's work contrasts vividly with Giotto's innovative depth and more expressive figures. One of the greatest painters of the 14th-century Sienese school was **Simone Martini**. This claim is evidenced by his graceful *Annunciation* (1333), painted for Siena's cathedral. Of the later Italian Gothic masterpieces, the *Adoration of the Magi* (1423) by Gentile da Fabriano is the most exquisite. Of the early Renaissance works, do not miss the large and exciting depiction of the *Battle of San Romano* (1456) by Uccello, or the paintings by Masaccio.

Detail of Botticelli's Birth of Venus

Among the most loved and reproduced of Renaissance paintings are the haunting *La Primavera* (The Allegory of Springtime; *c.*1480) by **Botticelli** and his renowned *Birth of Venus* (commonly referred to as 'Venus on the Half-Shell', *c.*1485). Botticelli's lifelike but theatrical *Adoration of the Magi* (under restoration until at least 2016) features portraits of the Medici family – Cosimo Il Vecchio, his son Piero Il Gottoso and grandsons Lorenzo Il Magnifico and Giuliano (standing smugly on the extreme left, a few years before his murder). Botticelli himself, in a yellow cloak and golden curls, gazes out on the far right.

In the same room is a huge 15th-century Flemish triptych by **Hugo Van der Goes**, *The Adoration of the Shepherds* (1478), which was painted for the Medici's Flemish agent, Tommaso Portinari.

The following room is devoted to **Leonardo da Vinci**. *The Baptism of Christ* (*c.*1474–5) was mostly the work of his great teacher, Verrocchio. Although only the background and the angel on the left were the work of the 18-year-old Leonardo, when Verrocchio saw how exquisitely his pupil had rendered the angel, he swore never to touch a paintbrush again. The *Annunciation* (1475) is entirely Leonardo's work, as is the *Adoration of the Magi* (1482).

The renovated **Tribuna** is an octagonal room that symbolises the four elements, which was commissioned by the Medici from Bernardo Buontalenti and completed in 1589. Visitors can view but no longer access the room and some of the major works of art have been moved permanently to the Red Rooms. Among the German masterpieces in the Uffizi, look out for *Portrait of His Father* (1490) and *Adoration of the Magi* (1504) by **Dürer**, and lifelike little portraits of Luther, his renegade wife, and a solid *Adam and Eve* (1526) by **Cranach.** Among the works of the 15th-century Venetian School is the strange, dream-like *Sacred Allegory*, painted about 1490 by Bellini. Its allegorical significance has never been fully explained.

Michelangelo's Dani Tondo

The Uffizi contains just one work by the great **Michelangelo**, a round oil painting showing the Holy Family, known as the *Doni Tondo* (1503–5). Firmly but humanly treated, it is the only known panel painting by an artist better known for frescoes and sculpture. The works by **Titian** include *Flora* (c.1515) and his celebrated, voluptuous nude, the Venus of *Urbino* (1538). At the time of writing, Room Nos 25–44, which include both the Michelangelo and Titian Rooms, are closed for temporary restoration. Check www.uffizi.com/second-floor-rooms-uffizi-gallery.asp information on current closures.

The Blue Rooms (Nos 46–55), opened in 2011, feature non-Italian art, mainly from the 17th and 18th centuries, and include portraits and self-portraits by Rembrandt. The Red Rooms (Nos 56–66), opened in 2012, display the great Medici family portraits by Bronzino. In the last room are some superb works by Raphael, including the famous *Madonna del Cardellino* (Madonna of the Goldfinch; c.1505) and a wistful self-portrait painted in Florence when he was only 23.

SCIENCE MUSEUM

The state-of-the-art **Museo Galileo ❽** (formerly the Museo di Storia della Scienza; www.museogalileo.it; daily 9.30am–6pm, Tue until 1pm) is a welcome change after over-indulgence in the arts. Renaissance Florence was an important centre of scientific research, and Cosimo II hired the best mathematicians, astronomers and cartographers from all over Europe and the Middle East. Beautifully engraved astrolabes and armillary spheres show the motion of the heavenly bodies. Other treasures include mahogany and brass reconstructions of Galileo's experiments and fascinating 15th- and 16th-century maps and globes that show how rapidly new discoveries were revolutionising our understanding of the world.

RENAISSANCE ARTISTS

Although the glimmerings of humanism can be seen in the works of Cimabue and Giotto, the Renaissance is said to have truly arrived when Brunelleschi submitted his design for the Baptistery doors in 1401. Although beaten by Ghiberti in the competition, Brunelleschi's relief of Abraham and Isaac is more dynamic and depicts the human drama of the story. Brunelleschi's most lasting legacy to the city is in architecture, especially his Duomo, Spedale degli Innocenti and the Pazzi Chapel, but he is also credited with the invention of measured perspective.

In sculpture, pride of place goes to Brunelleschi's friend Donatello (1386–1466), whose bas-relief on the plinth of his *St George* at Orsanmichele shows early use of perspective, and whose David was the first free-standing male nude since antiquity.

In painting, the Renaissance was ushered in by Masaccio (1401–28), with his solid, modelled human figures, followed by Paolo Uccello (1397–1475), master of perspective, and the melancholic Filippo Lippi (1406–69). In the realm of religious art, the outstanding figures were Andrea Verrocchio (1435–88), Leonardo da Vinci's teacher and a fine sculptor; Domenico Ghirlandaio (1449–94), famous for his frescoes; and the exquisitely lyrical Botticelli (1444–1510). The High Renaissance saw the arrival of three master artists who epitomise the period: Leonardo da Vinci (1452–1519), artist and scientist; Michelangelo (1475–1564), sculptor, painter and poet; and Raphael (1483–1520), a gifted painter.

THE BARGELLO AND SANTA CROCE

East of Piazza della Signoria is **Piazza San Firenze**. This small square is dominated by the towering Baroque facade of **San Firenze**, the seat of Florence's Law Courts.

THE BARGELLO

On the northern edge of the square is the forbidding, fortress-like Palazzo del Bargello, home of the **Museo Nazionale del Bargello** ❾ (www.uffizi.com; daily 8.15am–5pm, closed 1st, 3rd and 5th Mon of each month). This was Florence's original town hall and one of its earliest public buildings, begun around 1250. The Bargello served as the seat of the magistrates (*podestà*) responsible for law and order, and later housed the office of the Captain of Justice (*bargello*), the 16th-century equivalent of today's police commissioner. Today, the Bargello is to sculpture what the Uffizi is to painting, for it houses many Renaissance masterpieces.

Jason with the Golden Fleece, by Pietro Francavilla

The first room beyond the entrance is the **Sala Michelangelo,** where marks on the wall record the water level of the 1966 flood at 3m (9ft). Michelangelo was only 21 when he finished his early masterpiece, *The Drunken Bacchus*. He sculpted the marble *Pitti Tondo* of the

Virgin and Child eight years later in 1504, while working on his famous *David* (now in the Accademia). You will also find Michelangelo's 'other David', *Apollo*, sculpted 30 years after the original.

A 14th-century stone staircase leads to an arcaded loggia on the first floor, where you'll see Giambologna's series of remarkably lifelike bronze birds surrounding a marble figure representing *Architecture*.

The first-floor exhibits include Italian and Tuscan ceramics, old Murano glass, French Limoges enamels and astonishing, delicate engraved seashells. The 14th-century chapel contains frescoes painted by a pupil of Giotto. The man behind the kneeling figure on the right is said to be Dante.

Vasari Corridor

The Corridoio Vasariano is a graceful covered walkway built by Vasari in 1565, running from the Uffizi and over the Ponte Vecchio to the Medici's new headquarters in the Palazzo Pitti. It allowed Grand Duke Cosimo de' Medici to commute between the two without ever braving the elements or brushing shoulders with the populace. The corridor and its collection of portraits is now open to the public (Tue–Sun) but you must book your tour in advance at www.uffizi.com.

If you are pressed for time, head straight for the **Salone di Donatello**, which contains works by the sculptor that capture the spirit of early Renaissance Florence. Donatello's movingly human *St George* (1416) dominates the back wall of this impressively high-vaulted room. It was commissioned by the armourers' guild as their contribution to the exterior decorations of Orsanmichele. The sculpture's depth and sense of movement are generally believed to represent the first great sculptural achievement of the Renaissance.

Donatello's most important work – his bronze figure of *David* (1440–50) – is credited as the first free-standing nude statue of the Renaissance. In contrast to the 'modern' feeling of *St George*, his *David* has an antique and ambiguous sensuality about it, while the delightful bronze *Amore* (Cupid) is positively Roman in style. More personal and dramatic are the two marble versions of *St John the Baptist*.

Be sure to take a look at Ghiberti and Brunelleschi's original bronze panels (*The Sacrifice of Abraham*), designed for the Baptistery design competition of 1401; they're on the right wall towards the back of the room.

The Sala di Verrocchio on the second floor has Verrocchio's bronze David (*c.*1471), which may have been modelled on the sculptor's 19-year-old pupil, Leonardo da Vinci. Also on the second floor is the model for Giambologna's *Rape of the Sabine Women* in the Loggia dei Lanzi.

BADIA FIORENTINA

Across the street from the Bargello is the church known as the **Badia Fiorentina** (entrance on Via Dante Alighieri; Mon 3–6pm; free), with its graceful bell-tower; part Romanesque, part Gothic. Go inside for a moment to admire Filippino Lippi's delightful *Madonna Appearing to St Bernard*, on the left of the church as you enter.

From the southern end of Piazza San Firenze, take the Borgo dei Greci. This crosses **Via de' Bentaccordi**, one of the few curved streets in medieval Florence. It owes its shape to the fact that it once ran round the outside of Florence's Roman amphitheatre. At the far end of Borgo dei Greci you can see the black and white facade of Santa Croce.

PIAZZA SANTA CROCE

The vast expanse of **Piazza Santa Croce** formed one of the social and political hubs of Renaissance Florence, but is mostly a residential neighbourhood today. Lorenzo and Giuliano de' Medici used to stage lavish jousts here, and defiant Florentines turned

Santa Croce's neo-Gothic facade

out in force during the 1530 siege to watch or take part in their traditional football game (re-enacted here every summer). The buildings on the right-hand side of the square, with their cantilevered upper floors, were typical of the late medieval city.

The cavernous Franciscan church of **Santa Croce ⑩** (www. santacroceopera.it; Mon–Sat 9.30am–5.30pm, Sun 2–5.30pm, last entry 30 mins before closing; ticket valid for the entire complex and the Casa Buonarroti) started off in 1210 as a modest chapel, situated in the middle of a working-class district. Arnolfo di Cambio, the architect of the Palazzo Vecchio and the Duomo, drew up the plans for a larger church, which was completed in the 14th century. The interior, beneath its open roof-beams, is grandly Gothic, while the facade is 19th-century neo-Gothic.

The church is the last resting place of some of the most illustrious figures in Italian history, many of them born in Tuscany. Just inside the door on the right is the **tomb of Michelangelo,** designed by his first biographer, the 16th-century artist and

A statue of Dante Alighieri

architect Giorgio Vasari. The seated figures on the monument represent, from left to right, *Painting*, *Sculpture* and *Architecture*.

The next tomb on the right wall is that of Dante Alighieri. It lies empty, much to the dismay of Florence. A Florentine by birth, Dante was exiled for political reasons. His body lies in Ravenna, where he died; the city has never given in to Florentine pleas for its return (a statue to him stands just outside Santa Croce's main entrance). Farther along is the tomb of Niccolò Machiavelli (1469–1527), civil servant, political theorist, historian and playwright. Gioacchino Rossini (1792–1868), Florentine by adoption and the composer of *The Barber of Seville* and *The William Tell Overture*, is also buried here.

Opposite Michelangelo is the tomb of Galileo Galilei (1564–1642), shown holding the telescope that he invented. A plaque on the front of the Pisan's tomb depicts the four moons of Jupiter that he discovered with the use of the instrument. On the same side of the church, beside the fourth column from the door, lies sculptor Lorenzo Ghiberti, creator of the famous Baptistery.

A tranquil chapel in the left transept houses a coloured wooden Christ on the cross, carved by Donatello. His friend Brunelleschi mockingly dismissed the sculpture as 'a peasant on the cross'; Brunelleschi's answer can be found hanging in the Church of Santa Maria Novella. The honeycomb of family chapels on either side of the high altar contains a wealth of frescoes dating from the 14th to 16th centuries. To the right of the altar, in the **Bardi Chapel,** you will find Giotto's finest and arguably most moving works – scenes from the life of St Francis, painted around 1320. The adjoining chapel contains Giotto frescoes of the life of St John, commissioned by the Peruzzi, rich bankers who donated most of the money for the church's imposing sacristy. A fragment of tunic supposedly belonging to St Francis is displayed here.

CAPPELLA DEI PAZZI

The **Museo dell'Opera di Santa Croce** and, opposite, the **Cappella dei Pazzi** ⓫ (same times as the church) are also of interest. The once-tarnished reputation of the Pazzi family (resulting from the assassination of Giuliano Medici in the Duomo), was redeemed by their commission of the latter;

DANTE

Dante Alighieri, the father of Italian literature, was born in Florence around 1265. As a consequence of his Guelph allegiances, he was exiled from Florence for the last 19 years of his life and threatened with death by burning if he returned to the city. Though this sentence was repealed in 2008, his body remains in Ravenna and his tomb in Santa Croce lies empty.

Dante's immortal poetic work, *The Divine Comedy*, describes a journey through Hell and Purgatory to arrive at last in Paradise. One of the great landmarks of world literature, it juxtaposes divinely ordained political and social order with the ugly reality of the corrupt society that surrounded the poet in the early 1300s. Dante was the first to write his masterpiece not in the usual scholarly Latin, but in his everyday language. He thus established the Tuscan vernacular as the 'pure Italian' spoken today and used as the language of literature.

Battle of Lapiths against Centaurs, 1490–1492, by Michelangelo

a small but exquisite chapel. One of the earliest and most important Renaissance religious interiors, it was designed by Brunelleschi in 1443, and contains his glazed terracotta decorations of the four Evangelists and the tondos (circular works of art) of the 12 Apostles by Luca della Robbia. The former refectory houses a museum containing frescoes and statues that were removed from the church for preservation, but its greatest treasure is Cimabue's massive 13th-century painted crucifix. Restored after near-destruction in the 1966 flood, it hangs from heavy cables that can raise it out of harm's way at the push of a button.

CASA BUONARROTI

Close to Santa Croce are two more interesting museums. The **Casa Buonarroti** (Via Ghibellina 70; www.casabuonarroti.it; Nov–Feb Wed–Mon 10am–4pm, Mar–Oct Wed–Mon 10am–5pm), was bought by Michelangelo as an inheritance for his heirs. He lived for a short period of time in one of three small houses eventually combined to create the current residence. It contains letters, drawings and portraits of the great man, as well as a collection of 17th-century paintings illustrating his long, productive life. The exhibits include his famous sculptured relief the *Madonna of the Staircase*, completed before the artist was 16. His astonishing *Battle of the Lapiths and Centaurs* dates from around the same time.

THE HORNE MUSEUM

Situated near the river at Via de' Benci 6, the **Museo della Fondazione Horne** (www.museohorne.it; Mon–Sat 9am–1pm) is a superb little 15th-century palazzo, restored, briefly lived in, and eventually bequeathed to the city of Florence in 1916 by the eccentric Englishman Henry Percy Horne. On display is his priceless collection of Italian Renaissance art, ceramics and furniture. Museo Horne (tel: 055-244 661) is the meeting place for Saturday morning visits (10am, 11am and noon, Italian only) to the last home of the artist, architect and writer, Giorgio Vasari (1511–1574).

PIAZZA DELLA REPUBBLICA

To the west of Piazza della Signoria is the third major square of the *centro storico*, the grand **Piazza della Repubblica** ⑫, built on the site of the old Roman forum. Florence was capital of Italy from 1865–71, after which the capital was transferred to Rome. A jumble of medieval buildings was cleared during the 19th century to create the square, as part of the project to create a fitting capital for the newly independent state. The piazza's stylish cafés fill up at lunchtime with office workers from the surrounding banks and businesses, and there is usually live music on summer evenings.

If you leave Piazza della Repubblica by Via degli Strozzi, just before the end of the street on the left you will see the

Piazza della Repubblica, once the site of the Roman forum

massive walls of the **Palazzo Strozzi** (www.palazzostrozzi.org; daily 10am–8pm, Thu until 11pm), begun in 1489 as a private residence. Wrought-iron torch holders and rings for tethering horses are set in the masonry, but the cornice above the street remains unfinished, along with other details, since money for construction ran out after the death of Filippo Strozzi. The palace hosts three blockbuster exhibitions annually and is open year round with a café/bar and a permanent exhibition on the palace.

VIA TORNABUONI AND PIAZZA SANTA TRINITÀ

Via degli Strozzi leads to the pedestrianised **Via Tornabuoni** ⓭, one of Florence's main shopping streets, lined with the boutiques of the city's fashion houses. At the southern end of the road is the **Piazza Santa Trinità**. On the western side of the piazza is the fine 16th-century facade of the church of **Santa Trinità** ⓮ (daily 8am–noon and 4–6pm, Sun 8–10.45am and 4–6pm; free) by Bernardo Buontalenti. The Gothic interior comes as a complete surprise. It was built between the 13th and 15th centuries on the site of an older Romanesque church, the remains of which are still visible. Look for the late 15th-century Sassetti Chapel (second on the right from the chancel), with scenes from the life of St Francis by Ghirlandaio.

Outside the church, in the centre of the piazza, is the **Colonna della Giustizia** (Column of Justice), a granite pillar taken from the Baths of Caracalla in Rome. It was erected by Grand Duke Cosimo I de' Medici to celebrate his victory over a band of exiled Florentines anxious to overthrow him and re-establish a more democratic government.

Many wealthy families lived in the area, building impressive palazzos and sponsoring richly frescoed chapels. The exquisite, early 16th-century **Palazzo Bartolini-Salimbeni** and the 13th-century fortress-like **Palazzo Spini-Feroni** both stand on the piazza. The latter has been unofficially renamed the Palazzo Ferragamo, after the local family whose expanding empire of fashion and style is now located within the palazzo. The **Museo Ferragamo** (www.museoferragamo.it; daily 10am–7.30pm) in the basement displays lavish shoes created for the likes of Marilyn Monroe and Greta Garbo by the famous shoe designer, Salvatore Ferragamo.

PALAZZO DAVANZATI AND MERCATO NUOVO

East of Piazza Santa Trinità, on Via Porta Rossa, is the **Palazzo Davanzati** ⓯ (tel: 055-238 8610; www.uffizi.com; daily 8.15am–1.50pm, closed 2nd and 4th Sun, 1st, 3rd and 5th Mon of the month). The palazzo's museum gives a fascinating insight into life in medieval Florence. The dour exterior belies a splendid, colourful interior, especially the living quarters with their gorgeous wall hangings, frescoes and painted ceilings.

The Via Porta Rossa leads on to the **Mercato Nuovo**. A market has existed here since the 11th century; the main

Shopping for souvenirs in the Mercato Nuovo

attraction today is the profusion of stalls selling bags, belts, small leather goods and assorted souvenirs. The current arcade was built in 1547–51 for the sale of silk and gold.

ORSANMICHELE

North of the market, on Via della Calzaiuoli, is the unusual church of **Orsanmichele** 16 (Tue–Sun 10am–5pm; free). The original building was an open-sided loggia, like the Mercato Nuovo, and was rebuilt in 1337 by the silk guild for use as a market. It was converted to a church in 1380, and in the early 15th century the two upper storeys were added and used as an emergency granary. In the rear left-hand corner of the ceiling you can see the ducts through which grain was poured. Mystical and mysterious, the pillared interior is dominated by Orcagna's splendid 14th-century altarpiece, built around an allegedly miracle-working image of the Madonna.

Adopted by the city's wealthy merchant and craft guilds, the church's square, fortress-like exterior was embellished with

Gothicstyle niches and statues during the late 14th and early 15th centuries. Each guild paid for one of the 14 niches and commissioned a statue of its patron or favourite saint.

On the north side of the church is a copy of Donatello's *St George*. The original is in the Bargello. Commissioned by the armourers' and sword-makers' guild, this work was one of the first masterpieces of Renaissance sculpture. Particularly revolutionary at the time was the relief-work of St George killing the dragon, carved on a panel beneath the main statue.

Copies of Ghiberti's statues of *St Matthew* and *St Stephen* can be seen on the west side, opposite the impressive 13th-century **Palazzo dell'Arte della Lana**, once the headquarters of the powerful wool merchants' guild.

SAN LORENZO

This area to the north of the Duomo was home to the Medici dynasty for centuries and is the final resting place of all of the family's most important figures.

The rough-hewn dark stone structure of **San Lorenzo** ⑰ (www.operamedicealaurenziana.it; Mon–Sat 10am–5pm, Sun Mar–Oct only 1.30–5.30pm) looks like a huge Tuscan barn. Financed by the Medici, the prestigious project was built by Brunelleschi between 1425 and 1446, while its facade was to be completed by Michelangelo. He completed the interior but never delivered the planned external marble facings. The artist's model is on display at the Casa Buonarroti

A lucky pig

To the south of the Mercato Nuovo is *Il Porcellino* (the piglet), a 17th-century bronze statue of a boar, copied from a Roman marble original now in the Uffizi. Legend has it that if you stroke his nose and toss a coin into the fountain, you will return to the city.

museum. For once at least, 19th-century architects did not try to finish the job.

Florence's first entirely Renaissance church and one of Filippo Brunelleschi's earliest architectural triumphs (before he built the Duomo's cupola), the building was begun on the site of a 4th-century basilica. Cosimo Il Vecchio later had his palace built within sight of the church (the Palazzo Medici-Riccardi, with its entrance on Via Cavour). He liked to consider the Church of San Lorenzo as the Medici's parish church.

A door in the left wall of the church leads to the cloister and the stairs up to one of Michelangelo's architectural masterpieces, the **Biblioteca Medicea Laurenziana** (Laurentian Library, also accessible by a door to the left of the front entrance to the church; www.bml.firenze.sbn.it; Mon, Wed and Fri 8am–2pm, Tue and Thu 8am–5.30pm; combined ticket with San Lorenzo). A monumental staircase climbs to the reading room, graced with a splendid wooden ceiling and earthy terracotta floor. Commissioned by Pope Clement VII in 1524 to house a precious collection of Medici books and manuscripts, it was opened to the public in 1571 and is one of the world's most beautiful libraries.

The sober church of San Lorenzo was the burial site of many of the Medici. Cosimo Il Vecchio himself is in the crypt beneath the dome, while his parents are in the Old Sacristy, along with his two sons, Piero Il Gottoso and Giovanni, in a sumptuous porphyry-and-bronze tomb by Verrocchio. Donatello is buried in the left transept. A giant of early Renaissance art, he decorated the Brunelleschi-designed Old Sacristy.

THE MEDICI CHAPELS

San Lorenzo is best-known and most visited for the sumptuous Medici tombs, found in the **Cappelle Medicee** ⓲ (Medici

A splendid fresco inside San Lorenzo's dome

Chapels; www.uffizi.com; daily 8.15am–1.50pm, until 4.50pm in Apr–mid-Nov; closed 2nd and 4th Sun, 1st, 3rd and 5th Mon of the month). To visit them, you must go outside and walk around to the opposite end of the church, where you will find the entrance in Piazza Madonna degli Aldobrandini amid a jumble of stalls from the daily outdoor tourist market. From the crypt, filled with the tombs of minor family members, a staircase leads up to the **Cappella dei Principi**. This early 17thcentury Baroque extravaganza, added on after the completion of the New Sacristy, was intended to be the family burial vault to surpass all others. The workmanship of multi-coloured inlaid marble and semi-precious stones is astounding, even if by today's standards it looks a little over-the-top. Six huge sarcophagi bear the mortal remains of some lesser-known Medici (left to right from the entrance): Cosimo III, Francesco I, Cosimo I, Ferdinando I, Cosimo II and Ferdinando II.

Follow the stream of visitors to the main attraction, the **New Sacristy** (*Sagrestia Nuova*), reached via a corridor beside the stairs. This is an amazing one-man show by Michelangelo, who spent more than 14 years designing the interior and creating seven of the sculptures. Commissioned in 1520 by the future Pope Clement VII (the illegitimate son of Giuliano de' Medici) as a resting place for both his father (killed in the Duomo during the Pazzi conspiracy) and uncle (Lorenzo Il Magnifico), it also accommodated two then recently deceased cousins (Giuliano, Duke of Nemours, and Lorenzo II, Duke of Urbino). The walls behind the altar bear architectural sketches and markings, some of which are attributed to Michelangelo himself. Michelangelo worked on the Sacristy from 1521 to 1534; Vasari finished it in 1556.

Tomb of Lorenzo de Medici, by Buonarroti Michelangelo

The two more illustrious members of the Medici clan are buried to the right of the entrance, beneath Michelangelo's fine *Virgin and Child*, which is flanked by figures of the Medici patron saints, Cosmas and Damian. Ironically it was the two lesser cousins who were immortalised by Michelangelo with two of the most famous funeral monuments of all time. On the right stands an idealised, war-like Giuliano, Duke of Nemours, above two splendid figures symbolising *Night* (female) and *Day* (male), reclining on an elegantly curved sarcophagus. On the right, the unfinished face of

Day still shows the marks from Michelangelo's chisel, making the figure all the more remarkable. *Night* is accompanied by the symbols of darkness – an owl, a mask, the moon, and a sack of opium symbolising sleep. Opposite, a pensive Lorenzo, Duke of Urbino, sits above *Dawn* (female) and *Dusk* (male).

THE MERCATO CENTRALE AND PALAZZO RICCARDI

Just north of San Lorenzo, the busy, leather-scented street market of Via dell'Ariento and the late 19th-century covered **Mercato Centrale** add a dose of local colour. East of San Lorenzo on Via Cavour is the massive **Palazzo Medici-Riccardi ⓳** (entrance on Via Cavour; www.palazzo-medici.it; Thu–Tue 9am–7pm; entrance to the chapel is limited to 10 visitors every 7 minutes, so be prepared to queue). In 1439, Cosimo Il Vecchio, founder of the Medici dynasty, commissioned Brunelleschi's student Michelozzo to build the first home of the Medici clan, where they would live until 1540 when Cosimo I moved to the Palazzo Vecchio (see page 35) and then to the Palazzo Pitti (see page 69). Today it houses Florence's Prefecture, guarded by carabinieri (police).

The palazzo's ground-floor museum is often used for special exhibits, but its real attraction is the renovated Cappella dei Magi on the first floor. The chapel contains Benozzo Gozzoli's famous fresco, the *Procession of the Magi*, painted 1459–63. The work is a lavish pictorial record in rich, warm colours of everybody who was anybody in 15th-century Florence, including the whole Medici clan and a self-portrait of the light-blue-hatted artist.

SAN MARCO

North of the city centre, facing onto Piazza San Marco, is the Dominican church and monastery of **San Marco** (Mon–Sat 9.45am–4.45pm, Sun 2–5pm; free). The church houses one

Piazza San Marco

of Florence's most evocative museums: the **Museo di San Marco** (Mon–Fri 8.15am–1.50pm, Sat–Sun 8.15am–4.50pm, closed 2nd and 4th Mon and 1st, 3rd and 5th Sun of the month). The Florentine-born early-Renaissance painter Fra Angelico (1387–1455) lived here as a monk. Most of his finest paintings and frescoes, including the great *Deposition* altarpiece, can be seen in the Pilgrim's Hospice *(Ospizio dei Pelligrini)*, to the right of the entrance. Follow signs to the small Refectory (Refettorio), decorated with a vivid Ghirlandaio mural of *The Last Supper*, a favourite subject for monastery dining halls and one of seven in Florence.

The cloister bell resting placidly in the Sala della Capitolo has had a chequered career. Donated by Cosimo de' Medici, it was known as *La Piagnona* (The Great Moaner). In the 15th century, Girolamo Savonarola was the monastery's fire-and-brimstone preacher, prior and sworn enemy of the Medici. His puritanical supporters tolled the bell to alert the monks when an angry mob came to arrest him in 1498, earning them the nickname *I Piagnoni*. For its act of treason, the bell was condemned to 50 years of exile outside the city, and was whipped through the streets all the way out of town.

Upstairs in the dormitory, you can visit the monks' cells, each one bearing a fresco by Fra Angelico or one of his pupils.

His masterpiece, the famous *Annunciation*, is at the top of the stairs; another version can be found in cell No 3. At the end of the row to the right of the stairs are cells 38 and 39, once reserved for Cosimo de' Medici's meditations. At the farthest end of the dormitory are the former quarters of Savonarola.

The architect Michelozzo expanded the 13th-century monastery in 1437. His superb colonnaded library leads off the dormitory and is now used for rotating exhibits.

GALLERIA DELL'ACCADEMIA

At the east end of Piazza San Marco is a 14th-century loggia and the entrance to the Accademia di Belle Arti (Fine Arts). Founded by Cosimo I in the 16th century, the school was enlarged in 1784 with an exhibition hall and a collection of Florentine paintings. The entrance to the **Galleria dell'Accademia ㉑** (www.uffizi.com; Tue–Sun 8.15am–6.50pm) is on Via Ricasoli, south of the loggia.

The gallery's main attraction is its seven sculptures by Michelangelo, whose standout centrepiece is the 4.5m (15ft) *David,* perhaps the most famous sculpture in the Western world. Brought here from the Piazza della Signoria in 1873, it is displayed in a purpose-built domed room. Commissioned in 1501 as a symbol of Florence, upon its completion Michelangelo was just 26 years old. The balanced and harmonious composition and mastery of technique

Healing gardens

On the eastern side of San Marco is the delightful **Giardino dei Semplici**, also called the Orto Botanico (www.msn.unifi.it; Apr–mid-Oct Thu–Tue 10am–7pm, mid-Oct–Mar Sat–Sun 10am–4pm). Now part of the university, the garden was begun by Duke Cosimo in 1545 and was initially used to grow medicinal herbs, hence its name. Today tropical plants and Tuscan flora have been added to the collection.

Michelangelo's masterpiece

instantly established his David as a masterpiece. Cleaned in 2004, the marble has regained its original lustre, adding to its impact.

The other works here are the four *Prisoners*, providing a remarkable illustration of Michelangelo's technique as they emerge from the rough stone. He claimed that all his sculptures already existed within the block of marble, and that he only had to release them. These figures, apparently struggling to break out of the rough marble that holds them captive, offer a wonderful expression of his philosophy.

PIAZZA DELLA SANTISSIMA ANNUNZIATA

From the Piazza San Marco, a walk along Via C. Battisti leads to the **Piazza della Santissima Annunziata** ㉒, Florence's prettiest square and perhaps the finest example of Renaissance architecture and proportion in the city.

Brunelleschi probably designed the piazza, with graceful colonnades on three sides, when he built the square's Spedale degli Innocenti in the early 1440s. On the north side, the church of **Santissima Annunziata** (daily 7.30am–12.30pm and 4–6.30pm, Sun 8.45–9.45pm; free) was completed in 1481; its architect, Michelozzo, conformed to the piazza's original design, ensuring lasting harmony. The square's spacious feeling is added to by the two 17th-century fountains by Tacca, and Giambologna's equestrian statue of Grand Duke Ferdinando I.

The church entrance leads to an atrium decorated with frescoes by Andrea del Sarto, among others, from which a door opens into the extravagantly decorated interior. Immediately left of the entrance, the 15th-century shrine of the Annunziata shelters an old painting of the *Annunciation*, displayed only on special feast days and said in legend to be painted by a monk with the help of an angel. Reputed to have miraculous properties, it has been the object of pilgrimages and offerings for centuries.

THE FOUNDLING HOSPITAL

The **Galleria dello Spedale degli Innocenti** ㉓ (Mon–Sat 9am–6.30pm), on the east side of the square, exhibits 15th- and 16th-century sculptures and paintings belonging to Florence's Foundling Hospital (*Spedale degli Innocenti* means 'Hospital of the Innocents'). Built to Brunelleschi's design in the 1440s,

MICHELANGELO'S *DAVID*

The promising young Michelangelo had just completed the *Pietà*, now on display in Rome's St Peter's Basilica, when he was commissioned to sculpt his *David* in 1501. Of all his works, this masterpiece is most immediately associated with the Florentine master, who will forever be considered the Renaissance's most influential force. One detractor, the 19th-century Grand Tourist and essayist William Hazlitt, described it as 'an awkward overgrown actor at one of our minor theatres, without his clothes'. Those who come today to stand in quiet awe are more inclined to agree with D.H. Lawrence, who considered it 'the genius of Florence'. A life-size marble copy stands in front of the Palazzo Vecchio in the Piazza della Signoria, while a bronze replica anchors the hilltop Piazzale Michelangelo, where the magical sunset views over Florence are the same as those that influenced Florence's most famous son over 500 years ago.

it was the first foundling hospital in Europe. Note the 15th-century glazed terracotta roundels of swaddled babes by Andrea della Robbia on the arched façade. These are the 'della Robbia babies' that so appealed to Lucy Honeychurch, the heroine of E.M. Forster's novel *A Room with a View*. Under the northern end of the colonnade is the small door where abandoned babies were once left.

One of della Robbia's babies on the Spedale degli Innocenti

MUSEO ARCHEOLOGICO AND TEMPIO EBRAICO

The archway to the left/north of the Spedale leads out of the piazza and to the Via della Colonna and the **Museo Archeologico** 24 (Tue–Fri 8.30am–7pm, Mon, Sat and Sun 8.30am–2pm). Housed in what was once the palace of a grand duke, the museum holds important collections of ancient Egyptian, Greek and Etruscan art, especially the collection of bronzes that includes the famous *Chimera* (5th century BC). The superbly reconstructed Etruscan tombs in the gardens were damaged in the 1966 flood but have since been restored.

Beyond the Archaeological Museum, just off Via della Colonna on Via Luigi Carlo Farini, is the **Jewish Synagogue and Museum** (www.moked.it/firenzebraica; June–Sept Sun–Thu 10am–6.30pm, Fri 10am–5pm, Oct–May Sun–Thu 10am–5.30pm, Fri 10am–3pm). Florence's huge Jewish synagogue is easily recognised by its green, copper-covered dome. It was built in the Hispano-Moroccan style between 1874 and 1882 on the site of the ghetto, founded by Cosimo I in 1551. Ghetto, meaning 'slag' or 'waste', was first coined in Venice in the 1500s, referring to foundry on the Venetian island where Venice's Jews were confined. Segregation was the rule at the time in a hostile Europe where Jews, as non-Christians, were viewed as alien, and only some Italian city-states granted refuge.

SANTA MARIA NOVELLA

The first view of Florence for travellers emerging from the railway station is the slender campanile of Santa Maria Novella rising across the square. This is only the back view of one of Florence's greatest monastic churches; to appreciate the beauty of its multicoloured marble facade you must walk around into **Piazza Santa Maria Novella.**

SANTA MARIA NOVELLA

The cavernous church of **Santa Maria Novella** Ⓐ (www. chiesasantamarianovella.it; Apr–Sept Mon–Thu 9am–7pm, Fri 11am–7pm; Sat 9am–6.30pm, noon–6.30pm, Oct–Mar Mon–Thu 9am–5pm, Fri 11am–5.30pm, Sat 9am–5.30pm, Sun 1–5.30pm; last entry 45 mins before closing) was designed by Dominican architects in the mid-13th century. A small Dominican community still resides within its walls. In 1470 the architect Leon Battista Alberti completed the upper part of the bold, inlaid marble front in Renaissance style.

Walk beneath the soaring vaults of the 100m (328ft) tall nave to the cluster of richly frescoed family chapels surrounding the altar. The chancel is decorated with a dazzling fresco cycle by Ghirlandaio depicting *Scenes from the Lives of the Virgin and St John*, which was paid for by the wealthy Tornabuoni family. Ghirlandaio, Florence's leading 'social' painter of the late 15th

The Holy Trinity, by Masaccio

century, peopled his biblical frescoes with members of the Tornabuoni clan – one of whom was the mother of Lorenzo Il Magnifico – all dressed in the latest everyday fashions.

To the right of the altar are the **Filippo Strozzi Chapel**, colourfully frescoed by Filippino Lippi, son of the painter Fra Filippo, and the **Bardi Chapel**, with 14th-century frescoes. **The Gondi Chapel** to the left of the altar contains a Brunelleschi crucifix, a response to Donatello's 'peasant' crucifix in Santa Croce and his only work in wood. On the extreme left is the **Strozzi Chapel,** with 14th-century frescoes of *The Last Judgement, Heaven* and *Hell*. Its benefactors, of course, are depicted in Heaven.

The church's most striking work is Masaccio's *Trinity* (*c.*1427) on the wall of the left aisle. Famous for the first such handling of early perspective and a convincing illusion of depth, the fresco depicts the crucifixion in a purely Renaissance architectural setting, dramatically breaking from the established canons of religious art.

MUSEUM AND CLOISTERS

The renovation of Santa Maria Novella's **museum** (same hours and combined ticket with the church), arranged around the cloisters, added a new entrance from the station square, among other improvements. The great 14th-century cloister with its three giant cypresses is known as the **Chiostro Verde** (Green Cloister) after the greenish tint of the frescoes of the *Universal Deluge* by Paolo Uccello. Nearby the **Cappellone degli Spagnoli** (Spanish Chapel) is an impressive, vaulted chapter-house named in honour of Cosimo I's Spanish wife, Eleonora of Toledo. Gigantic 14th-century frescoes cover its four walls. The artist incorporated a picture of the Duomo complete with its cupola – 60 years before it was actually completed. Treasures from the monastery are housed in the large, vaulted Chapter House.

MUSEO MARINO MARINI AND CAPPELLA RUCELLAI

South of Piazza Santa Maria Novella, the Via dei Fossi – lined with antiques shops – leads down to the riverside **Piazza Goldoni**. A little way down Via dei Fossi on the left, Via della Spada leads to the **Museo Marino Marini** (www.museomarinomarini.it; Mon and Wed–Sat 10am–5pm). Set in the deconsecrated San Pancrazio church, the museum has an excellent collection of the 20th-century sculptor's work. Accessed from the museum is the Rucellai Chapel (same hours and ticket as museum), opened permanently to the public in 2013. Attributed to Alberti, this is a tiny scale model of the Church of the Holy Sepulchre in Jerusalem, with decorative and symbolic marble inlay.

Turtle tracks

Before leaving Piazza Santa Maria Novella, note the stone obelisks supported by Giambologna's bronze turtles. They marked the boundaries of horse races and chicken races common from approximately 1550–1850.

Ognissanti

OGNISSANTI

From Piazza Goldoni, Borgo Ognissanti leads towards the church of **Ognissanti** (All Saints; Mon–Sat 9am–noon, 4–5.30pm, Sun 4–5.30pm; free). The church dates from around 1250, contrary to the impression given by its fine 17th-century facade and the della Robbia glazed-terracotta relief over the doorway. Its builders, the *Umiliati* (Humble Ones), were a monastic community who, ironically, ran a remarkably lucrative wool business and were among the first to put Florence on the road to financial prosperity. The church contains Botticelli's *St Augustine*, and in the Refectory, Ghirlandaio's other famous *Last Supper (Cenacolo)* (Mon, Wed and Sat 9am–noon). The wealthy Vespucci family commissioned both pieces. The Vespucci family's most famous member was the navigator and cartographer, Amerigo, who lent his name to the New World. Several family members are buried here, along with the great Sandro Botticelli himself.

THE OLTRARNO

The district on the south bank of the river, called the **Oltrarno** (beyond the Arno), contains some of Florence's most characterful neighbourhoods.

PONTE VECCHIO

Florence's oldest bridge, the **Ponte Vecchio** ㉖ was the only one spared destruction in World War II. Its banks were bombed, as evidenced by the 1950s buildings at either end, but the bridge remained intact. The present bridge dates to 1345 and is lined with jewellers' and goldsmiths' workshops that overhang the river. From the terrace in its middle, you can look west towards the softly curved arches of the elegant **Ponte Santa Trinità**. One of the many bridges blown up by the retreating Germans in August 1944, Trinità was carefully reconstructed, exactly as Ammannati had designed it in the 16th century.

Via de' Guicciardini passes the church of **Santa Felicità** (Mon–Sat 9.30am–12.30pm, 3.30–5.30pm) on the way towards Piazza de' Pitti. Inside are two works by the Mannerist artist Pontormo (1494–1557), an *Annunciation* and a *Deposition*.

PALAZZO PITTI

On Piazza de' Pitti is the huge **Palazzo Pitti** ㉗. The Florentine merchant Luca Pitti, who wanted to impress his rivals, the Medici, built this palace as a symbol of wealth and power. Begun in 1457, it was continuously enlarged until the 19th century. Pitti died (together with his savings) in 1472, but the Medici were sufficiently impressed by his palace to buy it in 1549, enlarging it substantially. It then served as the official residence of the Medici (beginning with Cosimo I and his wife Eleonora of Toledo) and the successive ruling families of

Cascine Park

A 15-minute walk west along the river from Ognissanti will bring you to Le Cascine, a pleasant park that runs along the embankment west of the city for 3km (2 miles). Cascina means 'dairy farm', and that is what it was until it was acquired by Duke Alessandro de' Medici then laid out as a park by his successor, Cosimo I.

Florence until 1919, when it was bequeathed to the country. The palace and grounds contain five museums. There is a cumulative ticket for the Galleria Palatina and Galleria d'Arte Moderna, and another for the gardens and niche museums.

PALATINE GALLERY AND ROYAL APARTMENTS

The sumptuous **Galleria Palatina** and the **Appartamenti Reali** (Palatine Gallery and Royal Apartments; www.polomuseale. firenze.it; Tue–Sun 8.15am–6.50pm) are the main attraction of the Palazzo Pitti complex. The latter consists of 14 lavishly decorated rooms. Its name is misleading as the inhabiting families were not in fact monarchs. The former preserves the magnificent art collection of the Medici and Lorraine grand dukes, just as the owners hung them. It is a grand jigsaw puzzle jumbled by theme and personal preference rather than historical sequence. Priceless paintings decorate dazzling rooms, hung four-high amid gilded, stuccoed and frescoed decoration. It is the largest and most important collection of paintings in Florence after the Uffizi. There are superb works by masters such as Titian, Rubens, Raphael, Botticelli, Velázquez and Murillo, exhibited in grandiose halls adorned with ceiling paintings of classical themes, such as the Hall of the Iliad and the Hall of Venus.

THE MODERN ART, COSTUME AND SILVER MUSEUMS

The best of 19th- and 20th-century Italian art can be seen in the interesting **Galleria d'Arte Moderna** (Gallery of Modern Art; Tue–Sun 8.15am–6.50pm), on the floor above the Palatina. Here you can discover the exciting works of Tuscany's own Impressionist movement, the *Macchiaioli* (or 'spot-painters') of the 1860s. In 1999, 100 new paintings were added to the already fascinating collection. On the same floor is the **Galleria del Costume** (daily Nov–Feb 8.15am–4.30pm, Mar 8.15am–5.30pm, Apr–May, Sept and Oct 8.15am–6.30pm,

The Ponte Vecchio reflected in the Arno

Jun–Aug 8.15am–7.30pm; closed first and last Mon of each month, last entrance 30 minutes before closure), which showcases fashions from the 18th century to the present day.

Sixteen sumptuous rooms comprise the **Museo degli Argenti** (same hours as Galleria del Costume), which displays some of the Medici's most cherished jewellery, gold, silver, cameos, crystal, ivory, furniture and porcelain, including the priceless collection of 16 exquisite antique vases that belonged to Lorenzo Il Magnifico. The room in which they are displayed is the biggest surprise of all, with 17th-century frescoes that create a dizzying optical illusion of height and depth.

THE GARDEN AND THE PORCELAIN MUSEUM

Once you've seen the galleries, take a relaxing stroll in the delightful **Giardino di Boboli 28**, an Italian pleasure-garden of arbours and cypress-lined avenues dotted with graceful statuary, lodges, grottoes and fountains. The entrance to the gardens (same hours as Galleria del Costume), at the back of

The Grotto of Buontalenti, in the Boboli Gardens

the palace courtyard, leads to the amphitheatre, which has a fine view of the palace and the city beyond. In 2013, the garden was declared a Unesco World Heritage site.

Up the hill behind it are the Vasca del Nettuno (Neptune Fountain) and the Palazzina detta 'del Cavaliere', housing the **Museo delle Porcellane** (porcelain; same hours as Galleria del Costume). Off to the right, at the end of a long cypress avenue, is the Piazzale dell'Isolotto, an idyllic island of greenery, fountains and sculpture set in an ornamental pond.

Returning downhill, head right just below the amphitheatre to see the **Grotta di Buontalenti** (guided tours only, daily Apr–Sept 11am, 1pm, 3pm, 4pm and 5pm, Oct–Mar 11am, 1pm and 3pm). A fake grotto full of sculptures, it also contains the much-photographed statue of Cosimo I's court jester, depicted as a pot-bellied dwarf riding on the back of a turtle.

GIARDINO BARDINI

A footpath from the Giardino di Boboli leads to the Giardino di Bardini (same ticket as Giardino di Boboli). Restored and open to the public, the manicured gardens rise up in terraces towards Piazzale Michelangelo. Less crowded than the Boboli Gardens, they feature statues, grottoes, fountains and fine views over Florence. The gardens can also be accessed from Via dei Bardi, near the Museo Bardini (see page 74).

SANTO SPIRITO

Turn left out of the Palazzo Pitti and walk up to the nearby Piazza San Felice and then right along Via Mazzetta to see the attractive, tree-lined **Piazza Santo Spirito**. Arrive before 2pm to explore the piazza's morning fruit and vegetable market, or to watch the trade from one of the pavement cafés. On the second Sunday of each month an antiques market takes over.

The modest pale-golden facade rising above the back of the piazza is the church of **Santo Spirito** ㉙ (Mon–Tue and Thu–Sat 10am–12.30pm, 4–5.30pm, Sun 4–5.30pm), an Augustinian foundation dating back to the 13th century. The present church was designed by Brunelleschi and built in the second half of the 15th century. The bare, unfinished exterior conceals a masterpiece of Renaissance architectural harmony. The interior's walls are lined with 39 elegant side altars, while slender stone columns with Corinthian capitals, arches and vaulted aisles interplay to create an impression of tremendous space.

SANTA MARIA DEL CARMINE

Further west is the unpretentious church of **Santa Maria del Carmine**. The church houses some seminal Renaissance frescoes commissioned by the wealthy merchant Felice Brancacci. From 1425–27, a young Masaccio and his teacher Masolino worked on the decorations of the **Cappella Brancacci** ㉚ (tel: 055-276 8224; www.museicivicifiorentini.comune.fi.it; Mon and Wed–Sat 10am–5pm, Sun 1–5pm; maximum of 30 visitors are allowed in at one time, for only 15 minutes, advance booking required) at the end of the right transept. Masolino's own work is striking enough, but Masaccio's *The Tribute Money and The Expulsion of Adam and Eve from the Garden of Eden* raised the

Masaccio's Adam and Eve in the Brancacci Chapel

art of painting to an unprecedented level. His feeling for light and space, his dramatic stage-set figures, and the solidity of their forms were considered little short of an inspired miracle. Their creation heralded the arrival of the Renaissance, where nothing like them had been painted before. Sadly, Masaccio died at the age of 27, in 1428.

A devastating fire in 1771 somehow left the Brancacci frescoes intact, but elsewhere in the church you will see the late Baroque architecture and styling used to recreate the church. Opposite the Brancacci Chapel is the Corsini Chapel, a rare jewel of the Florentine Baroque style.

PIAZZALE MICHELANGELO AND SAN MINIATO AL MONTE

Back at the Ponte Vecchio, the Via dei Bardi leads east to the Piazza Santa Maria Soprarno. A little farther along is the lovely **Museo Bardini** ③ (www.museicivicifiorentini.comune.fi.it; Fri–Mon 11am–5pm). Antiques dealer Stefano Bardini created his palazzo over a church and monastery, incorporating fragments of the ancient buildings. He bequeathed the palace and his eclectic art collection to the city in 1923. After a 15-year restoration programme the palace was returned to its former glory and opened to the public. Among the highlights are Bernardo Daddi's monumental crucifix, a terracotta altarpiece by Andrea della Robbia, a *Madonna* that is attributed to Donatello and Pollaiuolo's *St Michael*. Bardini also created the nearby Giardino Bardini, also now open to the public (see page 72).

Continuing east along Via di San Niccolò and a right turn up Via San Miniato will bring you to Porta San Miniato, one of the few surviving gateways from the 14th-century city wall. On the other side of the wall, follow Via dei Bastoni parallel with the wall until you reach a set of stone steps on the right that leads straight uphill, passing through leafy gardens and interrupted occasionally by a switchback road. At the top of the series of steps is the **Piazzale Michelangelo** ㉜. If you cannot manage or face the climb, buses 12 and 13 run here from Ponte alle Grazie. The square was laid out in the 19th century and is dotted with reproductions of Michelangelo's sculptures, not to mention scores of tour buses and souvenir stalls. The views are absolutely marvellous; it is from here that all those classic postcard pictures of the rooftops of Florence are taken.

The church of **San Miniato al Monte** ㉝ (Mon–Sat 9.30am–1pm, 3–7pm, Sun 3–7pm; free), arguably the most beautiful in Florence and beloved by Florentines, enjoys a magnificent hilltop location above Piazzale Michelangelo. St Minias, an early Christian martyred during the 3rd century AD, is said to have carried his own severed head up to this hilltop and set it down on the spot where the church was later built. Rebuilt in the early 11th century, it is a remarkable example of Florentine-style Romanesque architecture. The superb green-and-white marble facade, visible from Florence below, contains a 13th-century mosaic representing

Artistic pilgrimage

It is said that Florentine artists young and old made pilgrimages to the Brancacci Chapel to marvel at and learn from Masaccio's achievement (stories recount visits by Michelangelo and Leonardo, who sat and sketched).

Christ flanked by St Minias and the Virgin Mary. The cool, mystical interior has all the splendour of a Byzantine basilica, with its wealth of richly inlaid marble and mosaic decorations. Note the painted wooden ceiling, and the nave's 13th-century oriental-carpet-like marble pavement.

Beside the church, the **Cimetero Monumentale delle Porte Sante** dates back to 1864, when burials in the historic centre of Florence were banned. Look for the tomb of Tuscan-born Carlo Collodi (born Lorenzini), the author of *Pinocchio*.

EXCURSIONS

Within easy reach of Florence are some of Tuscany's most impressive attractions, all accessible on a day trip. On the hills above the city is the village of Fiesole, and in the neighbouring Chianti district the spectacular towers of San Gimignano. A little farther afield are the modern cities of Pisa and Siena, both powerful city-states in their day, the latter a great rival to Florence. Like Florence, Pisa and Siena celebrated their success through patronage of the arts, evolving their own visual styles and amassing troves of artistic and architectural treasures.

FIESOLE

A winding road climbs for some 8km (5 miles) through the outlying neighbourhoods north of Florence to the charming little hilltop town of **Fiesole ③** (take the No. 7 bus from Santa Maria Novella railway station or Piazza San Marco). An ancient Etruscan stronghold and later a Roman settlement, it provides an escape from the city's summer heat and offers wonderful views over Florence and the Arno Valley.

PIAZZA MINO

The bus drops you in the central **Piazza Mino,** which has a market on Saturdays and a couple of pleasant cafés. Opposite the bus stop is Fiesole's cathedral. Founded in 1028 and completed during the 13th and 14th centuries, **San Romolo** (Apr–Oct daily 7.30am–noon, 3–6pm, Nov–Mar daily 7.30am–noon, 2–5pm; free) was totally restored in the 19th century, leaving it with a rather drab exterior. Its campanile, visible for miles around, dates back to 1213. A Byzantine atmosphere pervades the interior, which contains the Capella Salutati, with two works by Mino da Fiesole – a tabernacle showing the *Virgin with Saints*, and the tomb of Bishop Salutati.

East of the cathedral is the **Teatro Romano** and the **Area Archeologica** Ⓐ (daily Apr–Sept 10am–7pm, Mar and Oct 10am–6pm, Nov–Feb Wed–Mon 10am–2pm; combination ticket includes Bandini Museum). The well-preserved theatre dates from around 100 BC and seats some 2,500 spectators, with stunning views. Half original and half restored, it is the site of a popular arts festival held in July and August. Below the theatre

Roman theatre at Fiesole, Tuscany

are the remains of the Roman baths and a temple. A small but interesting archaeological museum is housed in a replica of the temple inside the entrance. Just opposite the site is the **Museo Bandini** (Apr–Sept Fri–Sun 10am–7pm, Mar and Oct 10am–6pm, Nov–Feb 10am–2pm) with a collection of paintings by the Italian Primitives.

From the square, follow the signs for the extremely steep but picturesque **Via di San Francesco,** which climbs to the church of **San Francesco** Ⓑ (daily Apr–Sept 9am–noon and 3–7pm, Oct–Mar 9am–noon and 3–6pm; free) and its tiny monastery. The views of Florence from the terrace below the church are gorgeous. The monastery, its quirky, free antiquities museum and peaceful little cloisters, are enchanting. A wooded park offers a choice of footpaths back down the hill.

BETWEEN FIESOLE AND FLORENCE

From the southwest corner of the Piazza Mino, the steep **Via Vecchia Fiesolana,** zigzags down the hillside towards Florence. Over the centuries various villas have been built here to take advantage of the breathtaking views, including the **Villa Medici,** built here in 1458–61 by Michelozzo for Cosimo de' Medici.

You rejoin the main road at the 15th-century Dominican church and monastery of **San Domenico** (daily summer 7.30am–12.30pm and 4.30–6.30pm, winter 8.30am–noon and 4–6pm; free). Fra Angelico took his vows here; his fine fresco of *The Crucifixion* adorns the Chapterhouse.

Just before the church, a right turn leads to the **Badia Fiesolana** (Mon–Fri 9am–5.30pm, Sat 9am–noon), which was Fiesole's cathedral until 1028. Rebuilt by Cosimo Il Vecchio in the 15th century, it is a gem of Renaissance architecture.

From San Domenico it is possible to catch the the No. 7 bus or enjoy the pleasant 4km (2.5-mile) walk downhill through the Mugnone Valley and back to central Florence.

Cathedral of Pisa in Piazza de Miracoli

PISA

Roughly 80km (50 miles) west of Florence lies **Pisa** ㉟, the birthplace of Galileo, and home of the fabled Leaning Tower. The city was a flourishing commercial centre and port during the Middle Ages, until the silting-up of the Arno estuary left it stranded 11km (7 miles) inland from the coast. The most conspicuous legacy of Pisa's wealthy and powerful past, and what everybody comes to admire, are the architectural wonders of the **Piazza dei Miracoli** (Square of Miracles), also known as the Piazza del Duomo. The miracles in question are the Duomo itself, the Battistero, the Camposanto and, of course, the cathedral's circular campanile, the Leaning Tower.

The centrepiece of the Field of Miracles is the white marble **Duomo** (Cathedral; www.opapisa.it; daily mid-Dec–Feb 10am–5pm, Feb 28–mid-Mar and Nov 10am–6pm, mid-Mar–Sept 10am–8pm, Oct–mid-Dec 10am–7pm; free). This was the most important and influential Romanesque building in Tuscany, and the first to use the much-copied horizontal

Pisa's most famous sight

'banding' of grey-and-white marble stripes. It was begun *c.*1063 and completed by the 13th century; the bronze doors facing the tower date from 1180. The striped decoration is repeated in the vast interior, which also boasts an ornate wooden ceiling. The cathedral's masterpiece, however, is the magnificent carved pulpit by Giovanni Pisano (1302–10), son of the famous sculptor Nicola Pisano. Opposite the pulpit is the 16th-century **Galileo Lamp,** whose workings inspired his theory of pendulum movement. The apse's dazzling mosaics depicting **Christ Pantocrator** were finished in 1302 by Cimabue.

The **Battistero** (Baptistery; www.opapisa.it; daily mid-Dec– Feb 10am–5pm, Feb 28–mid-Mar 9am–6pm, mid-Mar–Sept 8am–8pm, Oct 9am–7pm, Nov–mid-Dec 10am–6pm; combined ticket for visiting several Piazza dei Miracoli monuments) was started in 1152 but not completed until the 14th century. The sparsely decorated interior, famous for its excellent acoustics, contains a superb hexagonal pulpit carved in 1260 by Nicola Pisano, father of Andrea and Giovanni.

However, it is the world-famous, 57m (187ft) campanile of the cathedral, the **Torre Pendente** (Leaning Tower; www.opapisa.it; daily, Feb 28–mid-Mar 9am–6pm, mid-Mar–Sept 8am–8pm, Oct and mid-Dec–Jan 9am–7pm, Nov–mid-Dec and Feb

9.30am–6pm; combined ticket for visiting several Piazza dei Miracoli monuments), which really captures the eye, just as beautiful and delicate as carved ivory, and now leaning by 4.5m (15ft), though measurements vary. Begun after the Duomo and Baptistery in 1173, the campanile began to lean when only three of the eight storeys had been completed, since the shifting ground beneath the Campo is waterlogged sand – hardly ideal foundation material (the Duomo and Baptistery are also marginally off kilter). Various architects attempted to correct the lean as construction work continued, resulting in a slight bend by the time of the tower's completion in 1372. A remarkable engineering project has saved the tower from collapse.

On the north side of the piazza is the walled **Camposanto** (same hours as Baptistery; combined ticket for visiting several Piazza dei Miracoli monuments) a unique 13th-century, cloister-like cemetery filled with sacred soil brought back from the Holy Land. The walls were once covered with remarkable 14–15th-century frescoes, some by Benozzo Gozzoli. These were badly damaged during World War II bombing raids, and were removed to the **Museo delle Sinopie** (same hours as Baptistery; combined ticket for visiting more than one Piazza dei Miracoli monuments) in Piazza del Duomo. The **Museo del Duomo**, housed in a former 13th-century monastery in the Piazza del Duomo, shelters a wealth of artwork taken from the Duomo and Baptistery.

SIENA

The hilltop city of **Siena** ㊱, around 34km (21 miles) south of Florence, has retained its medieval character. Its walls enclose a maze of narrow, winding streets that have survived virtually unchanged since the 16th century and earlier. As you approach Siena along a road cut through a succession of undulating hills covered with a rich, reddish-brown soil, you will understand how the colour 'burnt sienna' came by its name.

The city itself is a wonderful marriage of brick and stone, all weathered reds and warm pinks. Imposing Gothic architecture prevails within the city walls, from the main square's early 14th-century Palazzo Pubblico, with its graceful and slender 97m (320ft) tower, the Torre del Mangia, to the grand zebra-striped cathedral and many fine palazzos.

PIAZZA DEL CAMPO

The heart of the city is the huge, sloping, fan-shaped **Piazza del Campo Ⓐ** (commonly known as Il Campo), where the Palio horse race (see box) takes place twice each summer. Siena's atmosphere of aristocratic grandeur befits the proud Ghibelline stronghold it once was. According to ancient myth, it was founded by the descendants of Remus (whose twin brother Romulus founded Rome), while in reality it was colonised by

SIENA'S PALIO

If you are in the region over the 2 July or 16 August, it's worth going out of your way to see the Palio, a traditional bareback horse race held in the Piazza del Campo since the 13th century.

After a stately hour-long parade of colourful pages, men-at-arms, knights and flag-twirlers dressed in 15th-century costumes, 10 fiercely competitive bareback riders, each representing a different *contrada* (city ward), battle it out during three wild laps around the dirt-covered piazza. The winning *contrada* is awarded the coveted Palio, a painted silken standard. The only rule is that the riders must not interfere with each other's reins; otherwise, anything goes – and often does.

No tickets are needed for the huge, emotional crowd on the campo, sweltering in the summer heat. Try to reserve a seat in the stands or a place on a balcony with a view, as the Campo is uncomfortable at best. However, tickets can be virtually impossible to obtain.

the ancient Romans under Augustus. This most stubbornly independent of Tuscan cities remained a republic for over 400 years, until it was defeated by Florence in 1555 and soon thereafter slipped into a centuries-long slumber.

The view from the Torre del Mangia

Within the Campo's **Palazzo Pubblico** ⓑ is the **Museo Civico** (www.comune.siena. it; daily mid-Mar–Oct 10am–7pm, Nov–mid-Mar 10am–6pm), where you can see Siena-born artist Simone Martini's early yet important frescoes of the *Maestà* (Madonna Enthroned; 1315), and the *Condottiere Guidoriccio da Fogliano* (1328) on his richly caparisoned horse. In the next room are local master Ambrogio Lorenzetti's impressive allegorical frescoes, *The Effect of Good and Bad Government* (1339), one of the largest medieval paintings of a secular theme.

PIAZZA DEL DUOMO

Almost all of historic Siena is closed to traffic. Wander freely through the picturesque, winding and hilly streets to the great Gothic **Duomo** ⓒ (www.operaduomo.siena.it; Mar–Oct 10.30am–7pm, Nov–Feb 10.30am–5.30pm; combined ticket with Museo dell'Opera del Duomo), perched atop Siena's highest point. Begun in 1196, it is visible from afar for its striking black and white striped exterior, a motif repeated in the city's coat of arms. The attractions within include the uniquely intricate inlaid marble floor, a splendid sculptured octagonal pulpit (1265) by Nicola Pisano, and Pinturicchio's colourful historical frescoes (1509) in the adjoining Piccolomini Library. A viewing balcony, La Porta del Cielo or Gateway to Heaven (tel: 057-728

6300; reservations only; extra charge), opened in 2013, affords spectacular views into the Duomo's interior and the city itself.

In the neighbouring **Museo dell'Opera del Duomo** (www. operaduomo.siena.it; same times as Duomo), the focal point is the splendid *Maestà* (1308) by local master painter Duccio. He is one of the leading Italian painters of Siena's important 13th- and 14th-century school of art, whose finest examples are on display in the city's art gallery, the **Pinacoteca Nazionale** (www. pinacotecanazionale.siena.it; Tue–Sat 8.15am–7.15pm, Mon and Sun 9am–1pm), housed south of the Duomo in the imposing Palazzo Buonsignori.

SANTA MARIA DELLA SCALA

Opposite the Duomo entrance is the **Santa Maria della Scala** Ⓓ (www.santamariadellascala.com; Mon, Wed, Thu and Fri 10.30am–4.30pm, Sat–Sun 10.30am–6.30pm). In its heyday this former pilgrim's hospital was one of the most important hospitals in the world. The vast complex, comprising the hospital and several floors of cellars, now functions as a cultural centre. Highlights are the Sala del Pellegrinaio (ground floor), with stunning frescoes illustrating the story of this hospital, Jacopo della Quercia's original sculpted panels from the Fonte Gaia (Fountain of Joy) in Siena's Campo and the archaeological museum.

SAN GIMIGNANO

The walled medieval town of **San Gimignano** ㉗ is one of Italy's most evocative. Strategically set on a hilltop, its skyline bristles with the angular outlines of traditional 12–13th-century Tuscan tower-houses. It was a matter of prestige to build the tallest tower possible, so at one point San Gimignano had over 70. Today just over a dozen remain; more than enough to make it the best-preserved (and most popular) town in Tuscany, and to earn it the proud name '*delle belle torri*' (of the beautiful towers).

Here you can stroll through streets and squares barely changed since Dante arrived as a Florentine envoy in 1300. The 12th-century **Collegiata** church (www.duomosangimignano.it; Apr–Oct Mon–Fri 10am–7.30pm, Sat 10am–5.30pm, Sun 12.30–7.30pm, Nov–Mar Mon–Sat 10am–5pm, Sun 12.30–5pm, closed second half of Jan and second half of Nov), with its plain-façade, is filled with impressive frescoes. The tiny **Cappella di Santa Fina** (1475) is decorated with elegant Ghirlandaio murals that depict San Gimignano's towers in the background. Santa

Medieval San Gimignano, the town of towers

Fina, only 15 years old when she died in 1253, was a local mystic who was adopted as one of the town's patron saints.

The 13–14th-century **Palazzo del Popolo** (town hall), with its 36m (117ft) tower, contains the **Museo Civico** and **Pinacoteca** (daily Mar 10am–5.30pm, Apr–Sept 9am–7pm, Oct 9.30am–5.30pm, Nov–Feb 11am–5.30pm). The **Torre Grossa** has a superb little courtyard, and unusual frescoes of hunting and courtly love.

Be sure to visit the 13th-century church of **Sant'Agostino** (Jan–Mar Mon 4–6pm, Tue–Sun 10–noon, 2–6pm, Apr–Oct daily 10am–noon, 3–7pm, Nov–Dec daily 10am–noon, 3–6pm). Its fresco cycle, painted in the choir by the 15th-century Florentine painter Gozzoli, depicts *Scenes from the Life of St Augustine*.

WHAT TO DO

SHOPPING

Since the Middle Ages, Florentines have held craftsmanship in high regard, and the city's elegant shops are famed for the quality of their merchandise, especially fashion and leather goods. It is one of Italy's best shopping destinations and one that promises good window-shopping.

Tourist and souvenir **markets** are held daily in the sprawling San Lorenzo area, and the less expansive Mercato Nuovo; the local market held every Tuesday morning in Cascine Park is the largest in Florence, selling everything from wine and cheese to clothes and shoes, giving a colourful insight into Florentine life.

FASHION

Some of the Italy's best designers started out in Florence, with many flagship stores still found in the city. Beautifully dressed shop windows compete for your attention along the expensive Via dei Tornabuoni, location of Gucci, Tod's, Ferragamo and Roberto Cavalli. The Florentine house of Emilio Pucci, with bold brightly coloured prints that evoke the 1960s, can be found on Via dei Tornabuoni 20-22r. Other good nearby hunting grounds are the Via della Vigna Nuova, the Via del Parione and Via Strozzi. Ferragamo fans should not miss the engaging shoe museum in the basement of the Ferragamo flagship store, Via dei Tornabuoni 4r–14r, while Gucci enthusiasts can visit the Gucci Museum in Piazza Signoria, opened in 2011, which tells the story of the designer and displays original pieces.

ANTIQUES AND REPRODUCTIONS

Antiques shops are clustered around two main areas: Via Maggio and the surrounding streets in the Oltrarno

Ponte Vecchio

Shopping hours

Shops traditionally close for a long lunch break (1/1.30–3.30/4pm), but an increasing number are open all day. Many shops don't open on Sunday or operate reduced hours, while some shops close on Monday morning. Many shops close for 7–10 days (minimum) on and around the 15 August for Ferragosto (Assumption Day), a national holiday and the start of the summer vacation season for most Italians, leaving the cities relatively empty and the coastal resorts packed. Shops may hang a sign reading 'chiuso per ferie' (closed for vacation).

and Borgo Ognissanti, west of the centre. Look out for old picture frames, antique jewellery, ceramics, statues, paintings and furniture; however you are unlikely to find a bargain. Framed 18th-century prints of Florence are good buys, especially in the shops around **Piazza del Duomo**. You can also look for unframed prints in the **San Lorenzo market.**

CERAMICS

Regional ceramic specialities include expensive, high-quality table china and brightly hand-painted ceramics of centuries-old Tuscan patterns and colours. Sbigoli Terrecotte (Via Sant'Egidio 4r; www.sbigoliterrecotte.it) has a good choice of beautiful hand-painted Tuscan ceramics, both traditional and contemporary designs.

GOLD AND SILVER

Designer gold jewellery is expensive (and almost always 18-carat), and most of it is now made in Arezzo. Every piece should be stamped, confirming that it is solid gold (ask to see the stamp, as minuscule as it may be). The ultimate place to window-shop is, of course, along the **Ponte Vecchio**, a bridge lined with dazzling, centuries-old jewellers' shops, each window more tempting (and densely stocked) than the last. Prices are not for the faint-hearted.

The work of Florence's unsung silversmiths is invariably beautiful and practical. Look for pillboxes, napkin rings, photo frames, cruet sets, sugar bowls and candlesticks.

INLAYS AND MOSAICS

The Florentine speciality of *intarsio*, the art of wood or semi-precious stone inlay, was perfected during the Renaissance. Some examples can be seen in the Uffizi, but the craft still flourishes. You will see modern interpretations and replicas of classic patterns for sale in **Lungarno Torrigiani, Via Guicciardini** and **Piazza Santa Croce**. Larger items such as tabletops are inevitably expensive and exorbitant to ship; small, framed 'naïve' pictures of birds, flowers, Tuscan landscapes or views of Florence are much less prohibitive.

A jewellery shop on Ponte Vecchio

LEATHER

Florence has been known for its quality leather goods since the Middle Ages. This is the hometown of the shoe and bag making greats Ferragamo and Gucci. San Lorenzo's famous market is awash with good-value leather stalls that sell everything from handbags and luggage to wallets and gloves. For top of the range quality and prices you should start with the designer boutiques in the Via de' Tornabuoni or the shops in streets around the Piazza della Repubblica.

The best buys in town are shoes and small leather goods: gloves, belts, purses, wallets and boxes, in all shapes and sizes and of varying quality. Handbags and outerwear can be gorgeous and tempting but do not expect bargains. The Santa Croce leather school (Scuola dei Cuoio; www.scuoladel cuoio.com) inside the monastery of Santa Croce, is a popular place to watch skilled Florentine leather-workers and to purchase their creations.

Special papers

For centuries Florence has been a major centre of hand-printing and bookbinding. In the past few decades these crafts have enjoyed a revival. Shops sell specialised stationery and items such as note-books, frames and albums covered in handmade marbled paper. Beautifully crafted creations include leather-bound books such as diaries, address books and journals.

PERFUMES

Florence is home to one of the world's oldest apothecaries. The **Officina Profumo Farmaceutica di Santa Maria Novella** (Via della Scala 16;

Florentine leather is famous for its quality

www.smnovella.it). Dominican monks, who used the premises to make herbal medicines, founded it back in the 14th century. When they turned to making perfume they attracted the patronage of Catherine de' Medici, assuring their future success. Today they still produce a wide range of traditional soaps and colognes, as well as a few innovations to keep up with the times. Purchases are beautifully packaged and sold out of their shop, within an old 14th-century chapel with a beautiful wooden and painted interior.

STREET MARKETS

The biggest and most popular market is **San Lorenzo**, which caters to both tourists and locals, and sells everything from football banners to sunglasses, with an ever-growing emphasis on touristy goods. You will find clothing (T-shirts, knitwear and woollen scarves), shoes and leatherwear, often at reasonable prices, but don't expect high-quality goods. Many stalls accept credit cards and travellers' cheques.

At its centre, stretching along Via dell' Ariento, is the late 19th-century structure that houses the **Mercato Centrale**, the city's largest and most colourful food market, bulging at the seams with just about everything produced in the surrounding Tuscan hills, from fresh fruit and vegetables to meat, fish and game. It is a great place for local colour, photo opportunities, insight into Florentine daily life and culinary heritage.

The **Mercato Nuovo**, or **Straw Market**, is conveniently located halfway between the Duomo and the Ponte Vecchio. Housed beneath a 16th-century loggia, a score of stalls sell leather bags and other miscellaneous souvenirs – a far less expansive (and less interesting) selection than its big-sister market at San Lorenzo.

A daily **flea market** operates in Piazza dei Ciompi, selling the usual mix of junk and bric-a-brac found in flea markets the world over. A more genuine antiques market is also held

A fruit and vegetable market stall at Mercato Centrale

in the same spot, and takes place on the last Sunday of each month. Antiques hunters can also visit the markets on Piazza Mino in Fiesole on the first Sunday of the month, or Piazza Santo Spirito on the second Sunday of the month.

Sant'Ambrogio morning market in Piazza Ghiberti sells fresh foodstuffs, including pasta, porcini mushrooms and other Italian specialities.

A huge weekly market every Tuesday morning in **Cascine Park** sells all kinds of goods to a far less touristy clientele (little English is spoken). This market is especially good for buying cheap clothes and shoes, or live chickens, whose days are numbered.

ENTERTAINMENT

There is always something interesting going on in Florence. Information on current events can be found on the weekly 'what's on' posters displayed throughout the city, and in the useful monthly publication *Firenze Spettacolo*, available from the tourist office and online at www.firenzespettacolo.it. There are also weekly entertainment listings in the weekend edition of the Italian-language *La Repubblica*.

THEATRE AND MUSIC

Florence's avant-garde Teatro dell'Opera di Firenze (opera house) in the Parco della Cascine, in Piazzale Vittorio Gui 1, was inaugurated in 2011. The theatre seats 1800, and also has concert halls and an open-air amphitheatre. It is the main venue for the Maggio Musicale Festival, which is held from late April to late June. Teatro Verdi (Via Ghibellina 99; www.teatroverdionline.it) is the venue for light opera, ballet, jazz and rock concerts. Tickets can be booked online.

Summertime alfresco concerts are held in the **Boboli Garden**. Organ recitals are presented in historic churches in September

The Maggio

The highlight of the musical year in Florence is one of Italy's principal music festivals, the Maggio Musicale (www.operadifirenze.it), held from late April to the end of June. It attracts some of the finest concert, ballet and operatic performers in the world, thanks in large part to the artistic direction of conductor Zubin Mehta.

and October, though sporadically in the colder winter months; the churches aren't heated. During June, July and August, nearby **Fiesole** holds the Estate Fiesolana festival of concerts, ballet, drama and film staged at the restored Roman amphitheatre. The opera season gets under way in December and runs until April, held mostly at the Teatro dell'Opera di Firenze.

An impressive chamber-music season is run by the **Amici della Musica** (www.amicimusica.fi.it) in the Teatro della Pergola.

NIGHTLIFE AND CINEMA

Florence is not renowned for nightclubs but it has plenty of bars, often with live music and/or an evening buffet for the price of an aperitivo. Of the currently fashionable and more attractive bars in the centre, try the arty bar-club **Dolce Vita** (Piazza del Carmine; www.dolcevitaflorence.com), Santa Croce's swank cocktail bar **Moyo** (Via dei Benci 23r; www.moyo.it), or the stylish Zoe (Via de Renai 13r; www.zoebar.it).

Most of the films screened in Florence are dubbed in Italian. The Odeon Cinehall, Piazza Strozzi 2 (www.odeonfirenze.com) shows some original-language films. During summer, the outdoor cinemas located along the Viale or on the hillsides offer a fun place to watch, with a welcome cool breeze.

SPORTS

Cycling. A national sport, as well as a great way to get around town. There are delightful rides in the surrounding countryside, too. Bikes are easy to hire (see page 116).

Football. If cycling is a national sport then football *(calcio)* is a national passion. The local team is Fiorentina (http://en.violachannel.tv). They play in Serie A at the Stadio Artemio Franchi near the Campo di Marte railway station. If you are in Florence on or around the feast of St John (late June), you may want to catch the Calcio in Costume, where a rough-and-tumble medieval version of the game is played in period costume.

Walking. There are endless options for great walks in the rolling green hills that surround the city. Visit Bellosguardo, Fiesole, the Certosa del Galluzzo monastery, Poggio Imperiale or the Arcetri observatory, set on the hill where Galileo gazed at the stars. All are within easy reach of the city, but you will certainly feel like you are in the Tuscan countryside. The tourist office can supply useful walking maps of the province.

At a concert

CHILDREN'S FLORENCE

Young children quickly tire of visiting museums and galleries, especially in the heat of summer. To keep things running smoothly, intersperse museum visits with ice cream from the city's many *gelaterie*, or visit the pigeons and cart horses that congregate in the Piazza della Signoria. The Boboli and Bardini Gardens and the Cascine are Florence's main parks, where children can let off steam.

Older children might enjoy the climb to the top of the campanile or the dome in the cathedral, if they can tolerate over 400 steps each. Consider a visit to one of the more offbeat museums, such as the 'Specola' Natural History Museum (www.msn.unifi.it), Via Romana 17, in the Oltrarno neighbourhood; the Anthropology Museum, Via del Proconsolo 12; the Museum of Mineralogy, the Botanical Museum and the Museum of Geology and Palaeontology, all at Via La Pira 4. The Stibbert Museum (www.museostibbert.it) is a little out of town, but the superb armour collections will spark their imaginations.

The Museo dei Ragazzi (Children's Museum; www.museoragazzi.it) is a scheme that has created interactive learning spaces for youngsters across Florence. There are multimedia stations across the historic centre, notably at the Palazzo Vecchio (Piazza della Signoria), where there are special tours for children, the Museo di Galileo and the Museo Stibbert. Highlights include encounters with historical figures such as Galileo and Vasari through lively narrations.

Children will enjoy climbing up the Duomo

CALENDAR OF EVENTS

February/March Shrove Tuesday: a low-key event in Florence, but nearby villages celebrate with fireworks and processions, the most notable of which are in Viareggio.

25 March Annunciation Day: celebrated with a small fair in Piazza della Santissima Annunziata.

March/April Easter Sunday Scoppio del Carro (Explosion of the Cart): In Piazza del Duomo an ox-drawn cart full of fireworks is set off by a mechanical dove that travels by wire from the cathedral's high altar at midday mass.

23 May Ascension Day, Festa del Grillo (Festival of the Cricket): fair in Cascine Park popular with children. Crickets in cages sold to be set free.

Late April to late June Maggio Musicale (Musical May; www.operadifirenze.it): prestigious programme of opera, ballet and concerts throughout the city by local and visiting artists.

16–17 June San Ranieri Historical Regatta, Pisa. The city's patron saint is celebrated by processions and races along the river.

Last Sunday in June Il Gioco del Ponte, Pisa. Twelve teams take part in a tug-of-war on the Ponte di Mezzo across the Arno.

June to August Estate Fiesolana: summer festival of music, ballet and theatre in the hilltop town of Fiesole.

24 June Feast of St John the Baptist, patron saint of Florence, celebrated with fireworks. Calcio in Costume: historical rowdy football game in 16th-century costume in Piazza Santa Croce, preceded by a lively, vibrant parade.

2 July and 16 August Palio di Siena: historic pageant and raucous horse race in Siena's beautiful Piazza del Campo.

10 August Festa di San Lorenzo: an outdoor celebration in Piazza San Lorenzo with live music and free lasagna served at 9pm.

7 September Festa della Rificolona (Festival of the Chinese Lanterns): evening procession with torches and lanterns, Ponte San Niccolò.

September to December Main opera season, with performances at the Teatro dell'Opera di Firenze, Piazzale Vittorio Gui 1.

EATING OUT

The emphasis in Tuscan cuisine is on straightforward, simply prepared *cucina povera* (meaning 'poor man's fare'). This comprises few seasonings, no elaborate sauces and the full flavour of primary ingredients from the bounty of Tuscany's fertile land.

The staples of the Tuscan kitchen are olive oil and bread. The olive oil produced in Tuscany is commonly extra virgin and is widely regarded as the finest in the world – dark green in colour, with a rich, peppery flavour. Tuscan olive oil is used in varying degrees on everything from soup to salad.

Your first taste of traditional crusty Tuscan bread will immediately tell you that it contains no salt (and is not eaten with butter). This tradition persists from the Middle Ages, when salt was a luxury item. Bread is served with every meal, and is a basic ingredient in many dishes.

WHERE AND WHEN TO EAT

The streets of Florence's historic centre are packed with cafés and bars where you can buy a beverage, snack or quick lunch to enjoy while standing at the bar or seated, or to take away. Sitting at a table will cost more, while sitting outside can be twice, or even three times, as expensive. Another option is the *tavola calda* (hot table), a self-service café where you can choose from a selection of pre-prepared dishes. These alternatives can be good for lunch, but those that cater to tourists usually offer mediocre, though often convenient, meals.

Restaurants range from an expensive *ristorante* to a

Local specialities

Italian cooking is essentially regional. Each of the country's 20 regions has its own unique specialities rarely found outside its boundaries, and similar dishes may have different names from region to region.

Piazza San Pier Maggiore

slightly more modestly priced family *trattoria*. Many restaurants still include a cover charge *(coperto)* and some a service *(servizio)* charge of 10–15 percent. If not, leave 10–15 percent for the waiter. Generally speaking the further away from the tourist attractions you go, the less expensive and less touristy the restaurants become. Reservations are recommended for more expensive establishments.

Breakfast *(prima colazione)* is usually included in the price of accommodation, and most hotels offers a buffet with rolls, fresh fruit, yogurt, cereal, homemade pastries, juice and coffee. Breakfast is usually served 7.30–10am.

Lunch *(pranzo, or colazione)* is served 12.30–2.30pm, though a limited number of places in Florence's centre will serve food throughout the entire afternoon. Cafés will always provide something to fill the gaps for a mid-afternoon snack (merenda).

Dinner *(cena)* begins at around 7.30pm, and is traditionally a fully-fledged affair of four courses.

WHAT TO EAT

As in the rest of Italy, restaurants tend to offer four main courses. The meal may start with an aperitivo (a drink accompanied by nibbles, such as olives) or antipasto (slightly heavier appetiser, such as a platter of cold meats). The first course is known as the primo (often soup, pasta and, occasionally, risotto), followed by the secondo (main course of meat, game or fish, usually grilled or roasted, and served unaccompanied), then dolci (dessert). Contorni (optional side dishes) are ordered separately and arrive with the entrée.

Bruschetta

ANTIPASTI

Certain antipasti are staples across Italy, such as antipasto misto (a table offering a mixed spread of starters, sometimes 'self-service') and melone con prosciutto (cantaloupe with thinly sliced, cured ham), which is best eaten during the summer when cantaloupe is in season. However, look out for Tuscan specialities such as prosciutto con fichi (prosciutto with fresh figs), Tuscan crostini (toast-rounds topped with chopped chicken livers, anchovies, capers, etc), or fettunta (toasted country bread rubbed with garlic and drizzled with olive oil). This is unfussy farmer's fare that rarely disappoints.

PRIMI

Florence has some excellent pasta options. Typically Tuscan are *pappardelle alla lepre* (broad noodles, usually homemade, with a tomato-based sauce of wild hare), as well as *spaghetti, penne* and *strozzipreti* (a 'priest strangler' of pasta, cheese and spinach, usually baked in the oven), dressed in a simple tomato sauce. Some restaurants will serve half portions *(mezza porzione)* of pasta upon request.

First-course non-pasta options are *polenta ai cinghiali* (a kind of cornmeal porridge dressed with a wild boar ragout); *panzanella* (a refreshing summertime salad of bread with tomato, red onion, basil and cucumber); *risotto ai funghi porcini* (slow-cooked rice with porcini mushrooms); and a speciality of *cacciucco* (a rich fish stew in red wine, tomato and peppers), which can pass as an entrée.

Traditional Tuscan soups include *pappa al pomodoro* (tomato soup thickened with bread), *ribollita* (a filling 'twice boiled' bread-based vegetable soup), or the staple *minestra* (a seasonal mixed vegetable soup, sometimes with pasta; variations are found throughout Italy).

SECONDI

Every visitor to Florence ought to try the famous *bistecca alla fiorentina*, a huge, charcoal-grilled T-bone steak, served with lemon or drizzled with olive oil. Each steak is at least 2cm (1in) thick and weighs 600–800g (21–28oz). Charred and crispy outside, they are rare and tender inside. The steak

Tagliatelle

is sold by weight and is not inexpensive. It is common for two people to share one *bistecca*.

Another classic Florentine main course is *trippa alla fiorentina*, which is tripe, cut into thin strips, gently fried in olive oil with onion. This can also be found at tripe stalls across the city.

Also on the menu are *fegato alla fiorentina* (sautéed liver with sage or rosemary), *arista* (roast loin of pork with rosemary and garlic), *fritto misto* (fried chicken and lamb with vegetables; this plate often includes calves' brains), *peposo* (beef stewed in a black pepper and tomato-based sauce) and *stracotto* (tender beef stewed with red wine and tomato).

Chicken turns up on the Tuscan dinner table, but Tuscans love game while in season, and they are more inclined to appreciate pigeon *(piccione)* and pheasant *(fagiano)*. You will find game roasted *(arrosto)*, stewed *(in umido)*, or simply grilled *(alla griglia)*. Simple preparation is always key in *cucina toscana*.

A few restaurants specialise in fish and seafood. Fish entrées from Tuscany's port city of Livorno might include *baccalà alla livornese* (a salted cod, tomato and garlic-based stew), but will simply follow the market's offerings.

CONTORNI

Bistecca Florentine

In Italy, vegetables *(verdure)* are ordered and charged for separately. Try *carciofini fritti* (fried baby artichokes), or grilled mushrooms such as porcini *(funghi or porcini alla griglia)*. Typical Tuscan side dishes include *fagioli all'uccelletto* (boiled white beans sautéed with tomato and sage), *fagioli al fiasco* (same ingredients, but stewed) and *fagioli all'olio* (boiled white beans, seasoned with olive oil, salt and pepper, and eaten at room temperature). *Insalata mista* (a mixed side salad) is usually good, but do not expect this to be included with any meal.

DOLCI

Desserts do not generally hold the same importance in Italy as they do in some other cuisines. Fresh fruit (*frutta di stagione*) or a fruit salad (*macedonia*) made of fresh fruit and ice cream (*gelato*) are the most common desserts.

A selection of luxurious gelati

Biscottini di Prato (also known as *cantuccini*) are hard almond biscuits that you soften by dipping into a glass of *vin santo*, a sweet dessert wine.

The summer heat in Florence can be overwhelming. A bewildering choice of delicious ice creams (*gelati*) can be found in the city's many *gelaterie*.

WHAT TO DRINK

Thirst-quenchers range from good Italian beers (*birra*) to summertime iced tea, peach- or lemon-flavoured (*tè freddo alla pesca or al limone*), a non-alcoholic bitter (*amaro*), freshly squeezed fruit juices (*spremuta*), iced espresso (*caffè freddo*), orangeade or lemonade (*aranciata or limonata*). There is always the alternative of mineral water (*acqua minerale*), still or

Frothy cappuccino

carbonated *(naturale or gasata)*. Florence's tap water is heavily chlorinated, but is safe to drink, albeit a little unpleasant.

The traditional **wine** of Tuscany is Chianti, probably the best known of all Italian wines. For many, Italian wine *is* Chianti – a basic pressing made from the Sangiovese grape. After a brief period of dormancy, Chianti production has experienced a resurgence of popularity and sales, and is once again considered one of Europe's premier wines.

Quality and prices vary, but the general standard is high. The official, Consortium-designated Chianti region stretches from Florence to Siena, entitling producers within the region to bear the *Gallo Nero* (black rooster) seal. Seals with a gold border indicate a *Chianti Classico Riserva*, meaning it was aged a year longer before bottling.

Consider joining an organised tour of the finest Chianti cellars. The tours take in Tuscany's gorgeous rural scenery, a few attractions on the way, and usually run from July to.

Tuscany produces a number of other superior reds,

including *Brolio, Vino Nobile di Montepulciano* and the fine aged *Brunello di Montalcino*.

Tuscan whites are unremarkable apart from the dry and elegant *Vernaccia di San Gimignano*.

End your meal with a small glass of *vin santo* (holy wine), a deep amber-coloured sweet wine, or choose from a local *grappa* (a distillate of grape must) or *limoncello*, a lemon-infused vodka served ice-cold.

An after-meal **espresso** *(un caffè)* is available in decaffein-ated form *(decaffinato)*. You can order it short, long, *macchiato* ('stained' with a dot of steamed milk) or just *normale*, black. Ordering *cappuccino* after 11am marks you as a tourist, but waiters are accustomed to the request of after-dinner cappuc-cinos by now (ordering coffee together with your dinner remains taboo). For a coffee that is not so strong, order a *caffè americano*.

PICNICS

For a breath of air, make up a picnic lunch and head for the hills of Fiesole, the Boboli or Bardini Gardens, or the terrace of San Mini-ato al Monte in the area of Piazzale Michelangelo. The only central square providing shade is Santo Spirito, near the Pitti Palace. Buy fresh fruit and bread from the market, then find one of the many Florentine delicatessens (*pizzicheria* or *salumeria*) or small grocers (*alimentari*) who stock a wide range of food and drink (including min-eral water and soft drinks), and often sell sandwich rolls (*panini*).

Delicious foods to try include *finocchiona*, Tuscany's fennel-stud-ded salami, and the wide range of Italian hams, salamis, *mortadella*, sausages and other cold meats. Cheese is also an important Italian picnic ingredient. Varieties to try include *stracchino, pecorino* (a tangy sheep's-milk cheese), *ricotta, provola* (smoked or fresh), *gorgonzola, parmigiano* and *grana*.

TO HELP YOU ORDER...

A table for one/two/three please **Un tavolo per una persona/per due/per tre**

I would like... **Vorrei...**

The bill please **Il conto per favore**

What would you recommend? **Cosa ci consiglia?**

...AND READ THE MENU

aglio garlic

agnello lamb

aragosta lobster

basilica basil

birra beer

bistecca beefsteak

burro butter

calamari squid

carciofi artichokes

cavallo horse

cinghiale wild boar

cipolle onions

coniglio rabbit

cozze mussels

fagioli beans

fagiolini green beans

finocchio fennel

formaggio cheese

frittata omelette

frutti di mare seafood

funghi mushrooms

gamberetti shrimps

gamberi prawns

gelato ice cream

insalata salad

lumache snails

maiale pork

manzo beef

melanzane aubergine

olio oil

olive olives

pane bread

panna cream

patate potatoes

peperoni peppers

pesce fish

piselli peas

pollo chicken

pomodori tomatoes

proscuitto ham

riso rice

salsiccie sausages

spinaci spinach

tonno tuna

uova eggs

verdure vegetables

vino wine

vitello veal

zucchini courgettes

zuppa soup

PLACES TO EAT

As a basic guide, we have used the following symbols to give an indication of the price of a three-course meal per person, excluding wine.

€€€€ over 80 euros   **€€€** 50–80 euros
€€ 25–50 euros   **€** below 25 euros

CENTRO STORICO (CENTRE)

Caffè Gilli €€ *Piazza della Repubblica 39r, tel: 055-213 896,* www.gilli.it. Founded over 250 years ago, the Caffè Gilli is the plushest of all the cafés on the Piazza Repubblica. The café is redolent of a bygone era (particularly the old-fashioned interior), with its silver service and impeccable waiters. A traditional favourite place to rendezvous, it is famous for its chocolates and especially its *gianduja*. **Caffè Paszkowski** (www.paszkowski.it; next door, closed Monday) is known for its summer evenings with live music.

Caffè Rivoire €€ *Piazza della Signoria 4r, tel: 055-214 412,* www.rivoire.it. This is arguably the most famous of all of Florence's historic cafés. It has a ringside seat in Florence's most picturesque piazza, overlooking Michelangelo's *David*. Outside seating is perfect for iced tea, light lunch and people watching. Thick, dark hot chocolate is a local wintertime tradition. Activity flutters around the bar; proper service at the inside tables attracts society ladies of a certain age, along with foot-weary tourists. Closed Monday

Cantinetta del Verrazzano € *Via dei Tavolini 18r, tel: 055-268 590,* www.verrazzano.com. Popular wine bar serving wines from the family vineyards in Chianti's Castello di Verrazzano. Baked breads from the wood-burning ovens make this a great place to stop for a *merenda* (snack) or light meal, with a dozen Tuscan wines by the glass.

Gustavino €€€ *Via della Condotta 37r, tel: 055-239 9806,* www.gustavino.it. The Tuscan cuisine here is creative without being too elaborate or over-fussy, and is served beautifully on large white plates. Look out for the speciality wine-and-food evenings they run. The Canova wine bar next door is open daily (noon–late) for similar dishes, and a choice of over 800 wines, but in a less formal atmosphere. Dinner only Monday to Friday, lunch and dinner Saturday to Sunday.

Ora d'Aria €€€ *Via dei Georgofili 11r, tel: 055-200 1619,* www.ora dariaristorante.com. Very handy for the Uffizi, this is a chic and highly popular little restaurant renowned for light contemporary variations on classic Tuscan fare. Expect dishes such as maccheroni soufflé, urchin risotto, broad bean soup with roast squid and steak tartare served with diced pear. Reservations recommended, at least 24hrs prior to arrival.

Il Vegetariano € *Via delle Ruote 30, tel: 055-475 030,* www.ilvegetariano.it. Florence, home of bistecca alla fiorentina, has few vegetarian restaurants, but this is certainly one of the best. It is cafeteria-style and crowded but is worth persevering with for the daily-changing dishes (both vegetarian and vegan), made with the freshest of vegetables. Interesting salads too – and all at very affordable prices.

SANTA CROCE (EAST)

Acqua al Due €€ *Via della Vigna Vecchia 40r, tel: 055-284 170,* www. acquaal2.it. Restaurant behind the Bargello known for its pasta: the signature dish is the pasta sampler plate with five varieties (with an occasional *risotto* thrown in). Second courses are available, but usually skipped for the dessert sampler. Locals, tourists, students and families share communal tables. Dinner only except Sunday, when lunch is also served.

Il Cibrèo Trattoria €€ *Via dei Macci 122r, tel: 055-234 1100.* Simple, *trattoria*-style restaurant that adopts a modern approach to classic Florentine dishes (i.e. no pasta) – *pappa al pomodoro* (a thick garlic-flavoured soup of bread and tomato), *piccione farcito con mostarda di frutta* (pigeon stuffed with spiced fruit), *palombo giovane alla livornese* (Livorno-style dove). Excellent desserts. The adjacent Cibrèo restaurant is widely acclaimed.

It shares the same kitchen, but is far more expensive and formal and requires reservations, often far in advance. Closed on Mondays.

Enoteca Pinchiori €€€€ *Via Ghibellina 87, tel: 055-242 777*, www.enotecapinchiorri.com. One of the best and most famous restaurants in Italy, with one of the world's greatest wine cellars and three Michelin stars. The menu blends French and Tuscan influences. Think sparkling chandeliers, silver cloches and impeccable service. Formal dress. Closed lunch on Sunday and all day Monday.

Finisterrae €€€ *Piazza Santa Croce 12; tel: 055-263 8675*, www.finisterraefirenze.com. A Mediterranean bar and restaurant with a choice selection of food from various cuisines. Start with tapas, followed by a Moroccan-style tagine or pasta dish. The ambience is relaxed and sultry, especially in the bar area. Daily 11am to 11pm.

Icche C'è C'è €€ *Via dei Magalotti 11r, tel: 055-216 589*, www.trattoriaicchecece.com. A rough translation of the name might be 'We've got what we've got' – in other words, ask what today's special is. Half way between the Bargello and the Arno this is an enjoyable and friendly establishment that serves good Florentine fare such as *ribollita and stracotto*. Closed Mondays.

Caffè Italiano € *Via Isola delle Stinche 11/13r, tel: 055-289 080*, www.caffeitaliano.it. An imposing earlyRenaissance palazzo houses the Caffè Italiano pizzeria, *osteria* and SUD. The former offers just three types of pizza, all delicious, the osteria serves good wines with carefully matched *salumi* (country-style salami and cheese) at lunchtime, and classic seasonal dishes in the evening, while SUD focuses on southern Italian cuisine, with a deli for take-aways.

Il Pizzaiuolo € *Via dei Macci 113r, tel: 055-241 171*, www.ilpizzaiuolo.it. Reservations are necessary at this hopping pizzeria, which in the evening offers just two seatings – at 7.30pm and at 9pm. A Neopolitan *pizzaiuolo* reigns over the wood-burning oven, turning out thick chewy-crusted pizza. There is a *trattoria* menu offering traditional Tuscan fare, but pizza is a must – at least as a table-shared appetiser to start the evening off. No credit cards. Closed Sunday and August.

SAN LORENZO AND SAN MARCO (NORTH)

Nerbone € *Piazza del Mercato Centrale, inside the market, tel (mobile): 055-219 949.* One of the most popular lunch spots in the area, Nerbone serves up a daily menu with local dishes featuring seasonal ingredients. The *bollito* sandwich, with boiled meat, is a favourite. Lunch only Monday to Saturday.

La Pentola dell'Oro €€€ *Via di Mezzo 24/26r, tel: 055-241 808,* www.lapentoladelloro.it. The recipes here are inspired by Medieval and Renaissance cookery. As well as being unique, this is one of the friendliest restaurants in the city. Chef Giuseppe Alessi is more than willing to explain the dishes. Dinner only Monday to Saturday, September to July.

ZàZà €€ *Piazza Mercato Centrale 26r, tel: 055-215 411,* www.trattoriazaza.it. Traditional Tuscan fare served at communal wooden tables frequented by tourists, market vendors and shoppers alike. Try the *crostini misti, ribollita* or the famous *bistecca.*

SANTA MARIA NOVELLA (WEST)

Buca Lapi €€€ *Via del Trebbio 1r, tel: 055-213 768,* www.bucalapi.com. In the cellar of the Palazzo Antinori, this charming restaurant serves one of the best *bistecca alla fiorentina* (enormous and beautifully grilled). As expected, being in the basement of the palazzo of one of Tuscany's best wine producers, it has an excellent range of wines. Dinner only Monday to Saturday.

Coco Lezzone €€ *Via del Parioncino 26/r, tel: 055-287 178,* www.cocolezzone.it. A small, popular, no-frills institution off the elite shopping strip Via Tornabuoni, serving classic Florentine food on small tables with red and white checked cloths. Try the tasty pasta with porcini mushrooms. Closed Sunday and Tuesday evening. No credit cards.

Sostanza Il Troia €€ *Via della Porcellana 25r, tel: 055-212 691.* Established in 1869, this casual *trattoria* near Piazza Santa Maria Novella offers minestrone, tripe, fried chicken and *stracotto*, but most people come for the acclaimed Ferragamo *fiorentina* (after all, this place originated as a butcher's shop). Don't miss the *frittata di carciofi* (artichoke omelette) in season. No credit cards. Closed Sunday and Saturday off-season.

OLTRARNO (SOUTH)

Antica Mescita San Niccolò € *Via di San Niccolò 60r, tel: 055-234 2836,* www.osteriasanniccolo.it. This *osteria* in Oltrarno does simple and cheap, but extremely good Italian food served up in a cheery, crowded atmosphere. Part of the eatery is set in a former chapel.

Bevo Vino € *Via di San Niccolò 59r, tel: 055-200 1709.* A lovely medium-sized *enoteca*, offering daily first and second courses, *carpaccio* and *bruschetta*. It has good wine and cheese selections and the service is friendly and knowledgeable. During the summer outdoor seating is available. Daily noon until late.

Borgo Antico €€ *Piazza Santo Spirito 6r, tel: 055-210 437,* www.borgoanticofirenze.com. Jam-packed trattoria known for great thin-crusted pizzas in a lively atmosphere. Young, often abrupt staff. There is a full menu as well, but grab a coveted outdoor piazza table and stick with a simple pizza, salad and carafe of house wine. Daily.

Filipepe €€€ *Via di San Niccolò 39r, tel: 055-200 1397,* www.filipepe.com. Filipepe is an elegant take on modern Mediterranean cuisine. Soft candle lighting, cove ceilings, and the bottles of wine lining the walls give each area a private, yet comfortable feel. Filipepe's menu offers a seasonal selection of typical ingredients, frequently from the southern regions of Italy, including different kinds of *carpaccio*, salads, soups and pastas. There is a small outdoor area for the summer. Daily noon to late.

Napoleone €€ *Piazza del Carmine 24, tel: 055-281 015,* www.trattorianapoleone.it. This colourful trattoria, with a quirky interior, is set in a quiet location near the church with a large terrace for summer dining. The regularly changing menu features Tuscan antipasti, champagne risotto, and plates of salumi and bistecca alla fiorentina. Dinner only, 7pm to 1am.

Osteria del Cinghiale Bianco €€ *Borgo S. Jacopo 43r, tel: 055-215 706,* www.cinghialebianco.com. Traditional dishes including hard-to-find *cinghiale* (wild boar) are even tastier in the medieval, mood-setting ambience accented by a few romantic niche tables. If *cinghiale* is not for you, there is a wide selection of simple classic Tuscan fare. Great choice for Sunday or Monday when most other restaurants are closed. Closed Tuesday and Wednesday.

Pitti Gola e Cantina € *Piazza de' Pitti 16, tel: 055-212 704,* www.pitti golaecantina.com. This is a great little *enoteca*, lined with shelving containing innumerable bottles of wine, many available by the glass. Pasta dishes and simple but tasty plates of *salumi* and cheese help the wine slip down. Daily 1pm to midnight.

Quattro Leoni €€ *Piazza della Passera, Via de' Vellutini 1r, tel: 055-218 562,* www.4leoni.com. One of the city's oldest restaurants, founded in 1550, the Four Lions is in a quiet square where diners can sit outside in summer. The traditional cooking is first class and there are new additions to the Tuscan menu on a daily basis. The fabulous signature dish is a pear and ricotta pasta in a creamy taleggio sauce.

Le Volpi e l'Uva € *Piazza dei Rossi 1, tel: 055-239 8132,* www.levolpi eluva.com. This superb little wine bar has a fantastic selection of Italian wines, including quite a number of little-known vintages from small producers. It also serves very tasty plates of cheese and *salumi*, as well as *schiacciatine* (thin flat bread) and hot focaccia topped with mushrooms and prosciutto. Monday to Saturday 11am to 9pm.

A–Z TRAVEL TIPS

A Summary of Practical Information

ACCOMMODATION

Florence offers a wide range of accommodation, from grand city palazzos and chic boutique hotels to B&Bs and pensione-style hotels. Private home stays are a fairly recent development in Florence but are a good way of experiencing closer contact with the locals while paying modest prices. Serviced apartments, or residences, are an attractive alternative to hotels. The Florence tourist board website (www.firenzeturismo.it) offers a wide array of accommodation. During the high season between March and October and at Easter and Christmas, Florence becomes very crowded and accommodation is at a premium. Book as far in advance as possible for these periods. Hotels are graded from one to five stars, but the star system reflects the extent of their facilities, rather than other qualities such as atmosphere, comfort or location.

If you find yourself in Florence without a hotel reservation, head for the tourist information/hotel reservation office in the Santa Maria Novella railway station (tel: 055-315 874; daily 9am–7pm); they will find you a room within your price range for a small fee.

Florence is expensive, on par at least with the major European cities. Prices rose further in 2011 when the new hotel tax was introduced. Guests are charged €1.5–5 a night according to the hotel's star rating. The cheapest hotels tend to be situated around the

Do you have any vacancies? **Avete camere libere?**
I'd like a single/double room **Vorrei una camera singola/
matrimoniale**
...with bath/shower/ private toilet **...con bagno/doccia/
gabinetto privato**
What's the rate per night/week? **Qual è il prezzo per una
notte/una settimana?**

Santa Maria Novella station area and the most expensive along the banks of the Arno. Breakfast is almost always included in the room rate, varying from an abundant buffet to just rolls and coffee.

Visitors should also consider staying just outside the city, in one of the country villas, or opting for the increasingly popular agriturismo – farm-stay holidays, which are often self-catering.

AIRPORTS

The largest international airport near Florence is the **Aeroporto Galileo Galilei** (www.pisa-airport.com) at Pisa, 85km (52 miles) west of Florence. British Airways (www.ba.com) flies there from London Heathrow and Gatwick. The budget airline easyJet (www.easyjet.com) flies direct to Pisa from Gatwick and Luton and Ryanair (www.ryanair.com) has a regular service from London Stansted.

A regular train service (www.trenitalia.com) links Florence to Pisa Centrale station, which can be reached from the airport by train (infrequent connections), bus or taxi. The simplest way is to take one of the coaches (www.terravision.eu or www.airportbusexpress.it) that run directly from Pisa Airport to Florence SMN station. The journey time is 1hr 10 mins. All tickets can be purchased at the airport.

Florence's small but growing airport, **Aeroporto Amerigo Vespucci** (www.aeroporto.firenze.it), is at Peretola, about 5km (3 miles) northwest of the city and is also known as Aeroporto Peretola. It handles domestic as well as a handful of European flights. From the UK British Airways (www.ba.com) fly direct, daily, from London Gatwick and London City Airport, Cityjet (www.cityjet.com) fly seven times a week direct from London City Airport, while Vueling (www.vueling.com) have some direct flights from Gatwick. A regular 20-minute bus service, 'Vola in Bus' (www.ataf.net), connects the airport with the SITA bus station in central Florence every 30 minutes or take a taxi for approximately €20–25 to midtown destinations (the journey takes approximately 15 minutes).

Another option is to fly to Bologna's **G. Marconi Airport** (www.

> Could you please take these bags to the bus/train/taxi, please? **Mi porti queste valige fino all'autobus/al treno/al taxi, per favore?**
> What time does the train for Florence leave? **A che ora parte il treno per Firenze?**

bologna-airport.it), 66km (41 miles) north of Florence. This route is served by British Airways, and these flights are often cheaper than on the Pisa route. Ryanair also flies to Bologna daily from the UK.

In Bologna a shuttle bus operates between the airport and the centre of Bologna. Trains run about twice hourly and the journey to Florence takes just over an hour.

B

BICYCLE HIRE

Vehicles have been banned from the city centre in an effort to reduce congestion and pollution. Cycling is becoming increasingly popular among Florentines and there are a growing number of bike lanes. However, cyclists need their wits about them to steer a course through the hordes of tourists around the Duomo. Bicycles can be hired from Florence By Bike, Via San Zanobi 54r, tel: 055-488 992, www.florencebybike.it or Alinari, Via San Zanobi 38r, tel: 055-280 500, www.alinarirental.com. Florence Town (www.florencetown. com) offer two-and-a-half-hour guided bike tours, from March to October daily, 10am and 3pm (from May to September also at 6pm).

BUDGETING FOR YOUR TRIP

Hotels (double room with bath, including tax and service, high-season rates): 5-star from €450, 4-star €250–450, 3-star €150–250, 2-star €120–150, 1-star under €120.

Meals and drinks: Light lunch €20–25, three course dinner with wine in a good establishment €50 plus, coffee €1.50–4, beer €2–4, glass of house wine €3–5, soft drinks €2–4. Waiter service will often cost twice as much as drinking at the bar.

Museums: Admission fees range from approximately €2 for the small church museums to between €7 and €15 for some of the major collections. There are reductions for all visitors under-18 (ID required), while entrance is free for all EU citizens under-18 and over-65. The Firenze Card is a museum and public transport pass (€72), valid for 72 hours and allowing admission to 72 museums (including the famous ones) in Florence and the area, plus unlimited travel on public transport. This is good value for keen sightseers and means that queues can be skipped. The majority of the state museums are free to the public on the first Sunday of every month.

C

CAR HIRE (See also Driving)

Forget about driving in Florence. Cars are banned from the centre and must be left in the car parks on the edge of the centre (www. firenzeparcheggi.it). Zones reading Zona Traffico Limitato (ZLT) mark the no-go areas. If you decide to hire a car to tour Tuscany, prices are around €250–300 a week for an economy car. In Florence, Via Borgo Ognissanti has a concentration of car-hire firms including **Avis** (Borgo Ognissanti 128r; tel: 055-213 629; www.avisautonoleggio.it), **Hertz** (Borgo Ognissanti 137r; tel: 055-239 8205; www.hertz.it), Europcar (Borgo Ognissanti 53; tel: 055-290 438; www.europcar.it) and Sixt (Borgo Ognissanti 96; tel: 055-277 6374; www.sixt.it). Cars can also be hired at Pisa and Florence airports. Booking from the UK is

I'd like to rent a car. **Vorrei noleggiare una macchina.**
...for one day/a week ...**per un giorno/una settimana**
I want full insurance. **Voglio l'assicurazione completa.**

generally much cheaper than hiring on arrival. Most firms take and hold a credit card payment, which serves as the charge on return of the car. The minimum rental age varies from 19–25. Tuscany is well served by motorways though tolls are expensive.

CLIMATE

Summer is often oppressively hot and sticky (the hills surrounding Florence capture the heat and humidity), while midwinter can be unpleasantly cold. The wettest months are October to April. The best times to visit are in spring and autumn, when temperatures are milder, but May and September have become extremely popular and crowded months to visit.

	J	F	M	A	M	J	J	A	S	O	N	D
°C												
max	9	12	16	20	24	29	32	31	28	21	14	10
min	2	2	5	5	12	15	17	17	15	11	6	3
°F												
max	48	53	59	68	75	84	89	88	82	70	57	50
min	35	36	40	46	53	59	62	61	59	52	43	37

CLOTHING

Wear light clothes in summer, a sweater or jacket for spring and autumn, then warm clothes, a waterproof jacket and umbrella in winter. Comfortable walking shoes highly recommended. Dress respectably if you intend to visit places of worship.

CRIME AND SAFETY

Petty crime is a major problem in Florence, particularly pickpocketing and the snatching of handbags and jewellery, especially in crowded areas, busy markets and on public buses. You should take all the usual precautions against theft – do not carry large amounts of cash, leave your valuables in the hotel safe. Never leave your bags or valuables in view in a parked car; and never leave your bags in a car boot overnight, even if out of sight. The only real danger is from possible pickpockets, especially in crowded areas, busy markets and on public buses. If you have a shoulder bag, wear it across your body – it is harder to snatch.

Any theft or loss must be reported immediately to the police; make sure you obtain a copy of the report in order to comply with your travel insurance. If your passport is lost or stolen, inform your consulate immediately.

I want to report a theft. **Voglio denunciare un furto.**
My wallet/passport/ticket has been stolen. **Mi hanno rubato il portafoglio/il passaporto/il biglietto.**
I've lost my passport/wallet/bag/purse. **Ho perso il passaporto/il portafoglio/la borsa/la borsetta.**

D

DISABLED TRAVELLERS

Florence is not an easy city for disabled travellers. Many of the more popular attractions are equipped with ramps for wheelchair access, but public transport is a problem, as are hotels, restaurants and most minor attractions. Unaccompanied visitors will usually experience some difficulty, so it is best to travel with a companion. Specialised tour operators or travel agencies offering customised tours and itineraries for those with disabilities include Flying Wheels Travel (www.flyingwheelstravel.com) and Accessible Journeys (www.disabilitytravel.com). Access-Able Travel Source (www.access-able.com) is another useful source. Those with a disabled symbol can obtain free entrance to the city centre limited zone (ZTL). For more information visit www.firenzeturismo.it.

DRIVING

Motorists planning to take their vehicle into Italy need a full driving licence, a Motor Insurance Certificate and a Vehicle Registration Document. Motorists must be over-18 to drive in Italy. If coming from the UK or Ireland, headlights must be adjusted for driving on the right and your number plate or a sticker must display the country that the car is registered in. The use of seatbelts in the front and back is obligatory; fines for non-compliance are stiff. A red warning triangle and reflective jackets must be carried in case of breakdown. Motorcycle riders must wear helmets. Documents must be carried at all times.

Driving conditions. Drive on the right, pass on the left. Give way to traffic coming from the right. Unless otherwise indicated speed limits in Italy are: 50kmh (30mph) in towns and built-up areas, 90kmh (55mph) on main roads and 130kmh (80mph) on highways.

Traffic police *(polizia stradale)*. Italian traffic police are authorised to impose on-the-spot fines for speeding and other traffic offences, such as driving while intoxicated (over 0.051 per cent alcohol in your bloodstream) or stopping in a no-stopping zone. All cities, and many towns and villages, have signs posted at the outskirts indicating the telephone number of the local traffic police headquarters or Carabinieri (see Police). Police have recently become stricter about speeding.

Accidents and Breakdowns. Should you be involved in a road accident, dial **112** for the *carabinieri (police)*. If your car is stolen or broken into, contact the Urban Police Headquarters *(Questura)* in Florence at Via Zara 2, and get a copy of their report for your insurance claim.

In the event of a breakdown dial **116**. This will put you in touch with the ACI (Automobile Club d'Italia), the national automobile organisation. About every 2km (1.5 miles or so) on the *autostrada* there's an emergency call box marked 'SOS'. Drivers of broken down vehicles are required to warn other vehicles by placing a red triangular danger sign at least 50 metres (150ft) behind the vehicle. Reflective jackets should be worn.

Driving in Florence. Taking a car to Florence is not worth the hassle. The centre of Florence (within the circle of avenues or **viali** that surround it on both sides of the River Arno) is a restricted ZTL area (*zona traffico limitato* – limited traffic zone). Between 7.30am and 6.30pm Monday–Saturday, only residents with special permits on their windscreens are allowed into this zone. CCTV cameras are placed at entrance points. If you need access to enter to offload baggage and passengers inform your hotel in advance of the registration number. This will be forwarded electronically to the relevant office. You must then go and park outside the ZTL. Motorist fines are very heavy and vehicles are frequently towed away.

Curva pericolosa Dangerous bend/curve
Deviazione Detour
Divieto di sorpasso No passing
Divieto di sosta No stopping
Lavori in corso Roadworks/Men working
Pericolo Danger
Rallentare Slow down
Senso vietato/unico No entry/One-way street
Vietato l'ingresso No entry
Zona pedonale Pedestrian zone
Ztl Limited traffic zone

E

ELECTRICITY

220V/50Hz AC is standard in Italy. An adaptor (*una presa complementare*) for Continental-style sockets will be needed; American 110V appliances also require a transformer.

EMBASSIES AND CONSULATES
In Florence:
South Africa (honorary consulate): Piazza Saltarelli 1, tel: 055-281 863
In Rome:
Australia (embassy): Via Antonio Bosio 5, tel: 06-852 721, www.italy.embassy.gov.au.
Canada (embassy): Via Zara 30, tel: 06-854 443 937, www.canada.it.
New Zealand (embassy): Via Clitunno 44, tel: 06-853 7501, www.nzembassy.com.
Republic of Ireland (embassy): Via Giacomo Medici 1, tel: 06-585 2381, www.ambasciata-irlanda.it.
UK (embassy): Via XX Settembre 80a, tel: 06-4220 0001, www.ukinitaly.fco.gov.uk.
US (embassy): Via Vittorio Veneto 121, tel: 06-46741, http://italy.usembassy.gov.

EMERGENCIES
If you don't speak Italian, find a local resident to help you or talk to the English-speaking operator on the telephone assisted service, tel: **170**.
Police **112**
General emergency **113**
Fire **115**
Paramedics **118**

Please, can you place an emergency call to the...?
Per favore, può fare una telefonata d'emergenza...?
police **alla polizia**
fire brigade **ai pompieri**
hospital **all'ospedale**

G

GAY AND LESBIAN TRAVELLERS

Florence is an easy-going destination for gay and lesbian visitors, with a lively local scene. The national gay rights organisation, Arcigay (tel: 055-012 3121, www.arcigay.it), has an active branch in the city (Via di Mezzo 39r) that can provide help and information.

GETTING THERE

By air. From the UK and US, there are scheduled flights from the major cities to the international gateway airports of Rome and Milan, where you can catch a connecting flight to Pisa (80km/50 miles from Florence) or to Florence itself. Non-stop flights from the UK connect London with Pisa and with Florence. Cityjet, (www.cityjet.com), flies direct to Florence from London City airport, British Airways, (www.ba.com), from Gatwick and London City airport and Vueling, (www.vueling.com), from Gatwick. Ryanair, (www.ryanair.com), offers low-cost, direct flights from London Stansted to Pisa and Bologna 100km (60 miles) from Florence. British Airways, (www.ba.com), and EasyJet, (www.easyjet.com), also fly to Pisa.

By rail. The train journey from London to Florence via Paris takes 15–18 hours: 2hrs 15 minutes from London (St Pancras) to Paris (Gare du Nord) on Eurostar, and another 13–15 hour journey from Paris (Gare de Bercy) on the overnight Thello Sleeper (www.thello.com), depending on the time of day you leave and the connection times. If you enjoy rail travel it is a pleasant journey, but it is not cheaper than flying with a budget airline. For international rail information, including train times, reservations and rail passes consult Rail Europe (tel: 0844 848 5848; www.raileurope.co.uk). Italian State Railways (www.trenitalia.com) offer fare reductions in certain cases. These are subject to variation, but there are almost always discounts for children and groups available. Ask at any railway station or go to the website for current information. These tickets can be purchased at home or in Italy.

GUIDES AND TOURS

For art and history tours contact Florence Guides (www.florence touristguides.com) or ArtViva (www.italy.artviva.com).

Some travel agencies and bus companies offer organised bus tours of the countryside around Florence, including excursions to San Gimignano/Siena or Pisa. Details can be obtained through your hotel, tourist information offices and local travel agencies.

> We'd like an English-speaking guide. **Desideriamo una guida che parla inglese.**
> I need an English interpreter. **Ho bisogno di un interprete d'inglese.**

H

HEALTH AND MEDICAL CARE (see also Emergencies)

EU citizens are entitled to the same medical treatment as an Italian citizen. Visitors will need to have a European Health Insurance Card (EHIC, www.ehic.org.uk) before they go. This covers medical treatment and medicines, although it is still necessary to pay prescription charges and a percentage of the costs for medicines. Note that the EHIC does not give any cover for trip cancellations, nor

> I need a doctor/dentist. **Ho bisogno di un medico/dentista.**
> It hurts here. **Ho un dolore qui.**
> a stomach ache **un mal di stomaco**
> a fever **la febbre**
> sunburn/sunstroke **una scottatura di sole/un colpo di sole**

does it provide repatriation in case of illness. For this you will need to take out private insurance. Canadian citizens are also covered by a reciprocal arrangement between the Italian and Canadian governments but US citizens are strongly advised to take out private health insurance. Remember to keep receipts so that you can claim a refund when you return home.

If you should need the services of an interpreter in a medical situation, contact the Associazione Volontari Ospedalieri, a group of volunteer interpreters who are always on call, and offer their telephone services free; tel: 055-234 4567.

Most pharmacies *(farmacie)* follow retail hours; the one in the Santa Maria Novella railway station stays open all night. At weekends or on public holidays, the addresses of pharmacists on duty are published in the newspaper *La Nazione* and are posted on every *farmacia* door. In Italy, pharmacists are able to diagnose and prescribe mild medication for which, elsewhere, you would normally need a prescription. If it is not a true emergency, make a visit to a pharmacist instead of the hospital.

There is an accident and emergency department in the city centre at Ospedale Santa Maria Nuova, Piazza Santa Maria Nuova, tel: 055-69381.

Tap water is safe to drink *(potabile)*. There are numerous old drinking fountains in Florence's parks and piazzas.

L

LANGUAGE

English is widely spoken in Florence, especially by the young, and you can get by without a word of Italian. However, it is polite to learn at least a few basic phrases.

Local people will welcome and encourage any attempt you make to use their language. When you enter a shop, restaurant or office, the greeting is always *buon giorno* (good morning) or *buona sera* (good afternoon/evening – used from around 1pm onwards). When enquiring, start with *per favore* (please), and for any service rendered say *grazie* (thanks), to which the reply is *prego* (don't mention it, you're welcome). Accompany a handshake with *piacere* (it's a pleasure). A more familiar greeting, used among friends, is ciao, which means both 'Hi' and 'See you later'.

M

MAPS
Tourist offices (see page 132) can supply free maps of the city centre and also have a useful map on their website (www.firenze turismo.it). One of the best commercially available maps of the city is by the Touring Club Italiano and is available in bookshops and at newsstands.

> I'd like a street plan of...**Vorrei una pianta della città...**
> I'd like a road map of this region. **Vorrei una carta stradale di questa regione.**

MEDIA
Newspapers and magazines *(giornali; riviste)*. The Florence-based national newspaper *La Nazione* provides national and international news, features and useful restaurant reviews and entertainment listings. The national paper, *La Repubblica*, also has a Florence edition. You can find newspapers in English at city-centre newsstands. English-language freebies, usually available from tourist offices, include the fortnightly *The Florentine* newspaper (www.theflorentine.net) for expats and tourists with excellent articles on Florence, Tuscany and Italy, and *Firenze Spettacolo* (www.firenzespettacolo.it), available from all newsstands, is the most informative monthly listings magazine.

MONEY

Currency. The official currency used in Italy is the euro (€). Notes are in denominations of 5, 10, 20, 50, 100 and 500 euros; coins in 1 and 2 euros and 1, 2, 5, 10, 20 and 50 cents.

Banks and currency exchange offices. Changing money in a bank can be time-consuming and opening hours are limited but they generally offer the best rates. Exchange offices, open all day and at weekends, can be found all over Florence, and at the railway station. Alert your bank at home that you will be using your card in Europe. Some banks refuse transactions if they notice large withdrawals abroad.

Credit cards and Travellers' Cheques. Most major credit cards, including Visa, American Express and MasterCard are accepted in hotels, restaurants and shops but some of the main galleries and museums only take cash. American Express has a full-service office for its clients on Via Dante Aligheri 22/r, near the Duomo. Travellers' cheques are widely accepted but you need a passport to cash them; transaction fees are high and queues at Italian banks notoriously slow.

I want to change some pounds/dollars/ travellers' cheques. **Desidero cambiare delle sterline/dei dollari/ 'travellers' cheques'**

Can I pay with this credit card? **Posso pagare con la carta di credito?**

Where is the bank/atm? **Dov'è il banco/bancomat?**

O

OPENING HOURS

Banks. These are usually open Monday–Friday 8.30am–1.30pm and 2.30–4pm. Exchange offices at airports and major railway stations are open until late in the evening and on Saturday and Sunday.

Churches. Generally closed for sightseeing at lunchtime, approximately noon–3pm or even later. They discourage tourist visits during Sunday morning services.

Museums and art galleries. Opening hours of museums and art galleries vary hugely and some change their hours from season to season. They are generally open from 8.15/9am–4.30pm, or in the case of some of the main sights, 7pm. Closing day is usually Monday. If Monday is a holiday, some museums and galleries close the following day. Some sights have restricted opening hours at weekends, especially Sundays. Pick up a printout of current opening hours from the tourist office or consult www.firenzemusei.it and www.polomuseale.firenze.it.

Shops. Although many of the large shops and supermarkets now remain open all day (no-stop or orario continuato), the majority still adhere to the decades-old Florentine tradition of closing for a long lunch and on Monday mornings (Wednesday afternoons for food shops). Generally, shop opening hours are: Monday 3.30/4–7.30/8pm and Tuesday–Saturday 8.30/9am–1/1.30pm and 3.30/4pm–7/8pm. Food shops tend to open earlier than this and close earlier, while clothes shops may do the opposite, often not opening until 10am. Some of the central Florentine shops remain open for some part of Sunday, but many still close on that day. Some shops close for August or at least for part of it and if you see a sign that says chiuso per ferie with dates, it indicates they are closed for a holiday and usually indicates the date when they will reopen.

P

POLICE

Florence's city police, the Vigili Urbani, handle traffic and parking and perform other routine tasks. While the officers rarely speak

English, they are courteous and helpful towards tourists. The *carabinieri*, a paramilitary force, wear light-brown or blue uniforms with peaked caps, and deal with more serious crimes and demonstrations. Outside town, the Polizia Stradale patrol the highways, issue speeding tickets and assist with breakdowns (see Driving).

Police Headquarters *(Questura)* and Stolen Vehicles Department, Via Zara 2, tel: 055-49771.

Carabinieri Regional Headquarters (the only station where you're likely to find someone who speaks English): Borgo Ognissanti 48, tel: 055-27661.

Polizia Stradale (Traffic Police), tel: 055-577 777.

Polizia Assistenza Turistica (Tourist Police), Via Pietrapiana 50r, tel: 055-203 911.

Where's the nearest police station? **Dov'è il più vicino punto di polizia?**

POST OFFICES

The central post office in Florence is at Via Pellicceria 3, just southwest of Piazza della Repubblica (www.poste.it). You can enter by a back door on Piazza Davanzati. Its opening hours are Monday–Friday 8.15am–7pm, Saturday 8.15am–12.30pm.

Most other post offices open from 8.15 or 8.30am–1.30 or 2pm Monday–Friday, until noon on Saturday and on the last day of the month. Stamps (francobolli) are also sold at tobacconists' shops.

Where's the nearest post office? **Dov'è l'ufficio postale più vicino?**
Have you received any mail for...? **C'è posta per...?**
I'd like a stamp for this letter/postcard. **Desidero un francobollo per questa lettera/cartolina.**

Post boxes are red – those marked *per la città* are for destinations within Florence, *per tutte le altre destinazioni* for all other destinations. The blue box is for express international post.

PUBLIC HOLIDAYS

Banks, offices, government institutions, most shops and many museums are closed on national holidays, as well as on the Florentines' local holiday on 24 June, commemorating the town's patron saint, San Giovanni Battista (St John the Baptist). During the long weekend of 15 August, almost everything in Florence (and Italy) closes.

1 January *Capodanno/Primo dell'Anno* New Year's Day
6 January *Epifania* Epiphany
25 April *Festa della Liberazione* Liberation Day
1 May *Festa del Lavoro* Labour Day
24 June *San Giovanni* Patron Saint of Florence
15 August *Ferragosto* Feast of the Assumption
1 November *Ognissanti* All Saints' Day
8 December *Concezione Immacolata* Immaculate Conception
25 December *Natale* Christmas Day
26 December *Santo Stefano* St Stephen's Day
Movable dates:
Pasqua Easter
Pasquetta/Lunedì di Pasqua Easter Monday

R

RELIGION

Italy is an overwhelmingly Catholic country, and the ideals and influence of the Vatican permeate Italian life and politics. While Florence is generally tolerant and accepting of other religions, religious and racial intolerance, especially against Roma and Muslims, is a growing problem in Italy. Mass is celebrated in English in the Duomo (every Saturday at 5pm), in the Church of St James (American Episcopal, Via Bernardo Rucellai 9, Sundays at 9am and 11am) and at St Mark's English Church (Via Maggio, 18, on Sundays at 10.30am).

In churches, shorts, miniskirts or bare shoulders are not considered respectable.

T

TELEPHONES

The country code for Italy is **39**, and the area code for the city of Florence is **055**. Note that you must dial the 055 prefix even when making local calls within the city of Florence. When calling from abroad you retain the initial zero on the local code. To make an international call from Italy, dial 00, followed by the country code (**44** for the UK, 1 for US and Canada, 61 for Australia, 353 for Ireland and 64 for New Zealand), then the area code and number.

The city has a decreasing number of telephone kiosks but almost every bar has a public phone. Telephone cards *(schede telefoniche), used in public kiosks,* can be bought from bars, tobacconists, newsstands and other outlets.

Mobile phones. The EU set a cap on roaming charges in May 2016, bringing down the price of mobile calls and texts within the EU, with a view to abolishing all charges by June 2017. If your phone is 'unlocked' (contact your provider for details) it is easy to buy a local pay-as-you-go sim card.

Give me coins/a telephone card, please. **Per favore, mi dia monette/una scheda telefonica.**

TIME DIFFERENCES

Italian time coincides with most of Western Europe – Greenwich

Mean Time plus one hour. In summer, an hour is added for Daylight Saving Time.

New York	London	**Florence**	Jo'burg	Sydney
6am	11am	**noon**	1pm	8pm

TIPPING

Many restaurants in Florence levy a coperto or cover charge and/or a service charge so tipping is not necessarily expected. If you want to give a tip, leave 10 percent in a restaurant and small change at a bar.

It is also customary to tip bellboys, doormen and lavatory attendants for their service. Taxi drivers do not expect a full 10 percent, and normal practice by Italians is simply to round up the fare.

Thank you, this is for you. **Grazie, questo è per Lei.**
Keep the change. **Tenga il resto.**

TOILETS

You will find public toilets in airports, railway and bus stations, museums and art galleries. The men's may be indicated by 'signori', the ladies' by 'signore'. All bars have toilet facilities, but buy a drink out of courtesy before you use them.

Where are the toilets? **Dove sono i gabinetti?**

TOURIST INFORMATION

The Italian State Tourist Office, or ENIT (www.enit.it), maintains offices in many countries, including:
Canada: 69 Yonge Street, Suite 1404, Toronto, Ontario, M5E 1K3,

tel: (416) 925 4799.

UK: 1 Princes Street, London W1B 2AY, tel: (020) 7408 1254.

US: 3800 Division Street, Stone Park, IL 60165, tel: (312) 644 0996; 686 Park Avenue, New York, NY 10065, tel: (212) 586 9249.

In Florence the Agenzia per il Turismo di Firenze (www.firenze turismo.it, email: firenzeturismo@cittametropolitana.fi.it) provides tourism information, with English-speaking staff, free maps, information on sights and free magazines in English. The €72 Firenze Card, a pass for 72 museums and free local transport, is available at the offices at the railway station and at Via Cavour.

Florence:
Piazza San Giovanni 1, inside the Bigallo Loggia, at the west corner of Via Calzaiuoli, (Mon–Sat 9am–7pm, Sun 9am–2pm).

Via Cavour 1r, north of the Duomo, tel: 055-290 832 (Mon–Fri 9am–1pm). This main branch covers both the city and the greater province of Florence.

Piazza Stazione 5 (across the square from the train station) tel: 055-212 245 (Mon–Sat 9am–7pm, Sun 9am–2pm). Be prepared for long queues. The 'tourist information' desk inside the train station is a hotel-booking service, tel: 055-212245.

For details on museums in Florence and opening times, see www.polomuseale.firenze.it.

Fiesole: Via Portigiani 3, tel: 055-596 1311, www.fiesoleforyou.it (Mon–Sat 10am–6pm).

Pisa: Piazza Vittorio Emanuele II 16 (close to the railway station), tel: 050-42291, www.pisaunicaterra.it (Mon–Sat 9am–7pm, Sun 9am–4pm).

San Gimignano: Piazza del Duomo, tel: 0577-940 008, www.san gimignano.com (daily Mar–Oct 10am–1pm and 3–7pm, Nov–Feb 10am–1pm and 2–6pm).

Siena: Piazza Duomo 1, tel: 0577-280 551, www.terresiena.it and www.comune.siena.it (Mon–Fri 10.30am–4.30pm, Sat–Sun 10.30am–6.30pm).

TRANSPORT

The centre of Florence is small enough to cover on foot; the easiest way to see the city given the traffic ban in the city centre, buses included. If you want to cross the town by public transport or visit peripheral sights there are fast and efficient electric buses (C1, C2, C3 and D) stopping near the main sights.

Buses. The local bus transport is operated by ATAF (www.ataf. net). Before you board, buy your ticket from tobacconists (tabacchi), newsstands, bars, ATAF offices or automatic ticket machines at main points throughout the city, including the main transport hub of Santa Maria Novella station. Tickets are €1.20 for a 90 minute journey, or 4 journeys for €4.70. A 24hr pass is €5, and you can also buy 3 (€12) and 7 day (€18) passes. All tickets must be stamped in the appropriate machines on board the bus at the beginning of the journey. You can purchase a ticket on board the bus but it will cost a good deal more. ATAF officials periodically conduct spot checks to make sure tickets have been stamped; they impose stiff fines on ticket-holders who have not stamped their tickets, no excuses accepted. Tickets are valid for 1, 2 or 24 hours, and you can make as many journeys as you like, as long as they begin within the period of validity (you only punch the ticket once, on the first bus you use). For details of timetables and routes, consult the website or ask at the ATAF information office outside the railway station on Piazza Stazione. For tourists the most popular routes going out of the centre are the No 7 from Piazza San Marco to Fiesole, and No 12 and 13 from the railway station to Piazzale Michelangelo.

A wide network of bus services operates throughout Tuscany, and fares are reasonable. Inter-city services are run by a number of different bus companies including Siena Mobilità (tel: 800-922 984, www.sienamobilita.it), which operates a rapid coach service to Siena roughly every half an hour in season, taking 75 minutes, and Lazzi (tel: 055-214637, www.lazzi.it), which runs a good service to Lucca.

Taxis. Taxis are white and can be picked up at ranks in the main city squares, or called by telephone (tel: 055-4390 or 055-4242) but not hailed. Fares are recorded on the meter, and there are extra charges for luggage, radio calls, Sunday and late-night trips. It is normal practice to round up the fare. There are fixed rates from Florence airport to the centre (currently €20).

Trains. The Italian State Railway, FS (Ferrovie dello Stato, www.trenitalia.com) has an excellent rail network. Florence's Santa Maria Novella station just behind the church of the same name was remarkably avant-garde for its time but the services are insufficient for today's needs and the station is undergoing a major revamp. There are regular services to Rome, Milan, Venice (to name but a few) and other European cities, plus fast services to Tuscan cities such as Arezzo and Pisa. In addition to the information office, there are a number of computerised information points, where you can get train times and fares from a touch-screen terminal. Prices are reasonable, particularly those for second-class travel. Be aware of the infamous Italian *sciopero* or train strikes (less frequent these days than in the past) that can last from a few hours to a few days.

Trams. Line 1 of the new controversial Tramvia network was opened in 2010, linking Santa Maria Novella to the suburb of Scandicci in the southwest of the city. This is the first of three planned inter-linking tramlines. Line 2 from Peretola (Florence) Airport to

When's the next bus/ train to...? **Quando parte il prossimo autobus/treno per...?**
single (one-way) **andata**
return (round-trip) **andata e ritorno**
first/second class **prima/seconda classe**
What's the fare to...? **Qual'è la tariffa per...?**
I'd like to make a seat reservation. **Vorrei prenotare un posto.**

Piazza della Libertà, via the railway station, was planned for completion in 2015 but work has not yet started. The third line, if it ever materializes, will run from Careggi to Bagno a Ripoli.

VISA AND ENTRY REQUIREMENTS

For citizens of EU countries a valid passport or identity card is all that is needed to enter Italy for stays of up to 90 days. Citizens of the US, Canada, Australia, New Zealand and South Africa require only a valid passport. A special visa or resident permit is required for stays of more than 90 days. Visa regulations change from time to time; for full information on passport and visa regulations check with the Italian Embassy in your country. To facilitate the replacement process in case you lose your passport while travelling, photocopy the first page of your passport twice; leave one copy at home and keep another with you, but separately from the passport.

Free exchange of non-duty-free goods for personal use is allowed between EU countries. Residents of non-EU countries can claim a refund for part of VAT (IVA in Italy) on purchases of more than €155 at stores participating in the VAT-refund scheme. Reclaim the VAT at the airport.

I've nothing to declare. **Non ho niente da dichiarare.**
It's for my personal use. **È per mio uso personale.**

WEBSITES AND INTERNET ACCESS

Websites are given throughout the book; of the general sites the most useful are:

www.enit.it – Italian Tourist Board

www.firenzeturismo.it – Florence Tourism
www.firenzemusei.it and www.polomuseale.firenze.it – collective sites for the major museums
www.ataf.net – local transport
www.visitflorence.com – packed with useful information, both cultural and practical on Florence and Tuscany
www.theflorentine.net – fortnightly English language paper with good articles on Florence, Tuscany and Italy.

Many hotels offer internet access and WiFi and there are a good number of internet cafés open until late. The Florence WiFi initiative provides one hour of free internet access in many locations around the city. The 72-hour Firenze Card comes with 72 hours of free WiFi at a number of hotspots in public places in central Florence.

Y

YOUTH HOSTELS

Contact your national youth hostel association before departure to obtain an international membership card. Hostelling International (www.hihostels.com) has one hostel in the area, in a converted villa on the outskirts of Florence, a 30 minute bus trip from the centre in Fiesole: Ostello Villa Camerata (Viale A. Righi 4; tel: 055-601 451). In the Tuscan countryside 30km (19 miles) from Florence is the Ostello del Chianti (Via Roma 137, Tavernelle Val di Pesa; tel: 055-805 0265).

There are several other hostels in Florence, some more centrally located than the Hostelling International one. Ostello Santa Monaca (Via Santa Monaca 6, tel: 055-268 338, www.ostellosanta monica.com) is in a 16th century convent not far from Santa Maria Novella Central Station. The more recent Plus Florence Hostel (Via Santa Caterina d'Alessandria 15, tel: 055-628 6347, www.plus hostels.com/plusflorence), complete with swimming pool, bar, terrace and flat-screen TVs, is located northeast of the station.

RECOMMENDED HOTELS

During the high season from April to November, accommodation in Florence is at a premium and you should try to book a room as far in advance as possible. The clement months of May/June and September are most popular, but in fact, reservations are always strongly recommended, especially for the smaller, lower-priced hotels. With lots of local conventions and trade fairs throughout the year, Florence can often fill unexpectedly in off months. However, if you do arrive in Florence without a reservation, the ITA office at Santa Maria Novella railway station will find a room for you (see page 114). Prices can drop considerably outside high season and it is worth asking what discounts are available.

As a basic guide, the symbols below indicate published rack rates per night for a standard double room with bath, including service, VAT and breakfast. Note that the prices do not include the Florence hotel tax, introduced in 2011. The charge is €1.5–5 per person per night, according to the hotel's number of stars. Thus a couple staying for four nights in a 4-star hotel would be taxed an extra €36, payable in cash only at the end of the stay. The charge is for a maximum of 7 nights, and children under 12 are exempt.

€€€€	over 300 euros
€€€	170–300 euros
€€	120–170 euros
€	under 120 euros

CENTRO STORICO (CENTRE)

Tornabuoni Beacci €€€ *Via dei Tornabuoni 3, 50123 Florence, tel: 055-212 645,* www.tornabuonihotels.com. A classic Florentine pensione-style hotel located on an upper floor of a 14th-century palazzo sited on the city's premier designer-lined shopping street. Old-fashioned elegance with a homely atmosphere.

Brunelleschi €€€€ *Piazza Santa Elizabetta 3, 50122 Florence, tel: 055-27370,* www.hotelbrunelleschi.it. Built on Roman foundations, this hotel has its own small medieval museum, and incorporates the adjoining Torre della Pagliazza into the premises – all on its own tiny little piazza in the shadow of the Duomo.

Helvetia & Bristol €€€€ *Via dei Pescioni 2, 50123 Florence, tel:* 20-3829 8081; www.niquesatravel.com. A small but grand hotel, with antiques and paintings scattered around the rooms and hallways. The sumptuous rooms have wonderful views and the marble-clad bathrooms are a treat. As well as a pretty winter garden, the hotel has a good restaurant.

Hermitage €€€ *Vicolo Marzio 1, 50122 Florence, tel: 055-287 216,* www.hermitagehotel.com. Romantic and central – reach out and touch the Ponte Vecchio. Housed in a 13th-century tower and invitingly decorated with oriental runners and potted palms. A top-floor alfresco breakfast terrace offers sweeping views.

NH Porta Rossa €€€ *Via Porta Rossa 19, 50123 Florence, tel: 055-271 0911,* www.nh-hotels.com. The family-run Porta Rossa hotel in an ancient palazzo was taken over by the Spanish chain NH Hotels, but manages to retain at least some of its old Florentine charm. Rooms are good value for a 4-star in the centre.

Torre Guelfa €€ *Borgo Santissimi Apostoli 8, 50123 Florence, tel: 055-239 6338,* www.hoteltorreguelfa.com. On an ultra-central cobbled side street, this early Renaissance palazzo was built around a medieval tower with breathtaking 360-degree views. Most room have canopied beds.

SANTA CROCE (EAST)

Locanda Orchidea € *Borgo degli Albizi 11, 50122 Florence, tel: 055-248 0346,* www.hotelorchideaflorence.it. There are only a handful of rooms in this budget hotel, housed very close to the Duomo, in the 12th-century palazzo in which Dante's wife was born. Furniture is old and quirky, and showers and baths are communal but the place has bags of character and the windows are huge, making the rooms light and airy. Four of the seven rooms overlook a peaceful garden. Closed for most of August.

Plaza Hotel Lucchesi €€€-€€€€ *Lungarno della Zecca Vecchia 38, 50122 Florence, tel: 055-26236,* www.hotelplazalucchesi.it. Elegant and friendly hotel overlooking the river (river-view and terraced rooms must be specially requested), a few blocks east of the Uffizi.

SAN LORENZO AND SAN MARCO (NORTH)

Casci €€ *Via Cavour 13, 50129 Florence, tel: 055-211 686,* www.hotel casci.com. Simple, tastefully renovated rooms in a 15th-century building that was once the home of composer Rossini. Run by an amiable family, and an easy stroll from the Duomo.

Cimabue € *Via Benifacio Lupi 7, 50129 Florence, tel: 055-475 601,* www.hotelcimabue.it. Set in a quiet residential section just outside the centre, this 3-star hotel has a charming setting with hospitable hosts. A leisurely half-hour stroll to the Duomo.

Four Seasons Firenze €€€€ *Borgo Pinti 99, 50121 Florence, tel: 055-26261,* www.fourseasons.com/florence. This über-luxurious palazzo hotel is stunning, with frescoed ceilings, sumptuous furnishings and delightful gardens. None of this is cheap but staying here is certainly doing Florence in style. Its Il Palagio restaurant has been awarded with one Michelin star.t.

Il Guelfo Bianco €€€ *Via Cavour 29, 50129 Florence, tel: 055-288 330,* www.ilguelfobianco.it. In a 15th-century palazzo just north of the Duomo, the hotel is stylishly furnished with original antiques combined with contemporary art.

Loggiato dei Serviti €€€ *Piazza della SS Annunziata 3, 50122 Florence, tel: 055-289 592,* www.loggiatodeiservitihotel.it. The name recalls the 16th-century Servite monastery once housed in this palazzo with loggia, set on a beautifully proportioned Renaissance piazza. Vaulted ceilings and imaginative design make each room unique.

Mario's €€ Via *Faenza 89, 50123 Florence, tel: 055-216 801,* www.hotelmarios.com. Two blocks from the railway station, this decades-old favourite is impeccably maintained, owned and managed with warmth. Loyal clients keep coming back.

Monna Lisa €€€-€€€€ *Borgo Pinti 27, 50121 Florence, tel: 055-247 9751*, www.monnalisa.it. In a landmark medieval palazzo, with original wooden ceilings, red-brick floors and lots of historical character. Rooms are generally small, the preferred (quieter) ones overlooking a central garden. Easy walk to both Duomo and Santa Croce.

Regency €€€€ *Piazza M. d'Azeglio 3, 50121 Florence, tel: 055-245 247*, www.regency-hotel.com. A refined 19th-century-style palazzo, attractively distinguished with antiques and a much-respected restaurant, situated on a leafy, quiet piazza in a residential corner of the city just east of the centre. Quite a walk to get there.

Residenza Johanna 1 € *Via Bonifacio Lupi 14, 50129 Florence, tel: 055-481 896*, www.johanna.it. One of a set of great value-for-money residences across the city. Set in a residential area to the north of the centre, the rooms are comfortable and nicely decorated, but there are few hotel frills; not all rooms have attached baths. A do-it-yourself breakfast kit is provided in each room.

SANTA MARIA NOVELLA (WEST)

Boscolo Hotel Astoria €€€ *Via del Giglio 9, 50123 Florence, tel: 055-239 8095*, www.boscoloastoria.hotelinfirenze.com. Fine old Florentine palazzo, part of which dates from the 13th and 14th centuries, offering gracious rooms. Centrally located, equidistant to the Duomo and open-air market of San Lorenzo.

Baglioni €€€ *Piazza Unità Italiana 6, tel: 055-23580*, www.hotel baglioni.it. A dignified, well-run hotel just across the square from the railway station. A turn-of-the-20th-century bastion with a roof-terrace restaurant offering fantastic views.

JK Place €€€€ *Piazza Santa Maria Novella 7, 50123 Florence, tel: 055-264 5181*, www.jkplace.com. This chic and luxurious design hotel is tucked into the corner of Piazza Santa Maria Novella. The very elegant interiors contain works of art and classic designer furniture and lighting. The suites and penthouse are particularly impressive, and the terrace bar is also wonderful.

Palazzo dal Borgo €€€ *Via della Scala 6, 50123 Florence, tel: 055-216 237*, www.hotelpalazzodalborgo.it. Formerly the Hotel Aprile, this has been renovated into an elegant four-star hotel. More appealing than most hotels near the station, it is an ex-Medici palace complete with frescoes, a pleasant breakfast room and pretty courtyard.

St Regis €€€€ *Piazza Ognissanti 1, 50123 Florence tel: 055-27161;* www.stregisflorence.com. On the Arno, the 5-star St Regis (formerly the Grand) reopened in 2011 after a major revamp. Expect polished service, luxurious guest rooms, gourmet cuisine and fine river views – with prices to match.

OLTRARNO (SOUTH)

Annalena €€ *Via Romana 34, 50125 Florence, tel: 055-222 402*, www. annalenahotel.com. Tasteful hotel on first floor of a historically important palazzo from the 14th century; many rooms share a terrace overlooking a lovely private garden. Located across from the Pitti Palace and Boboli Garden.

Lungarno €€€€ *Borgo S. Jacopo 12, 50125 Florence, tel: 055-2726 4000*, www.lungarnocollection.com. The only hotel directly on the (south) banks of the Arno, with half of its renovated rooms overlooking the Ponte Vecchio. The hotel was founded by the Ferragamo family, local scions of style and fashion. Some rooms are housed in an adjacent 15th-century tower.

FIESOLE

Il Salviatino €€€€ *Via del Salviatino, Firenze 50137, tel: 055-904 1111*, www.salviatino.com. Following a 60 million euro restoration of a palatial 15th century villa, Florence's most luxurious hotel recently opened in the lush Fiesole hills, high above the city. Sumptuous rooms feature 19th century frescoes, Renaissance art and silver candelabras. Guest rooms, including grand and opulent suites, are all individually furnished. Set in 11 acres of gardens and orchards with infinity pools, health club, spa and spectacular views of Florence.

INDEX

Berlitz POCKET GUIDE

FLORENCE

Fifteenth Edition 2016

Editor: Tom Fleming
Author: Patricia Schultz
Head of Production: Rebeka Davies
Picture Editor: Tom Smyth
Cartography Update: Carte
Update Production: AM Services
Photography Credits: Britta Jaschinski/Apa Publications 90, 103, 104; Getty Images 4TC, 4MC, 5T, 5TC, 5MC, 5MC, 6TL, 7M, 7MC, 9, 11, 14, 15, 20, 22, 26, 28, 40, 44, 48, 50, 54, 58, 74, 86, 89, 91, 99, 100, 101; iStock 5M, 6TL, 6ML, 7M, 8L, 9R, 13, 16, 19, 30, 33, 35, 36, 38, 62, 71, 79, 80, 83, 92, 102; News Pictures/REX/Shutterstock 95; Public domain 42; Shutterstock 4ML, 4TL, 5M, 7T, 7TC, 8R, 47, 57, 60, 64, 66, 68, 72, 96; Steve McDonald/Apa Publications 52, 85; SuperStock 77; TopFoto 25
Cover Picture: Corbis

Distribution
UK, Ireland and Europe: Apa Publications (UK) Ltd; sales@insightguides.com
United States and Canada: Ingram Publisher Services; ips@ingramcontent.com
Australia and New Zealand: Woodslane; info@woodslane.com.au
Southeast Asia: Apa Publications (SN) Pte; singaporeoffice@insightguides.com
Hong Kong, Taiwan and China:
Apa Publications (HK) Ltd; hongkongoffice@insightguides.com
Worldwide: Apa Publications (UK) Ltd; sales@insightguides.com

Special Sales, Content Licensing and CoPublishing
Insight Guides can be purchased in bulk quantities at discounted prices. We can create special editions, personalised jackets and corporate imprints tailored to your needs. sales@insightguides.biz;
www.insightguides.biz

Contact us
Every effort has been made to provide accurate information in this publication, but changes are inevitable. The publisher cannot be responsible for any resulting loss, inconvenience or injury. We would appreciate it if readers would call our attention to any errors or outdated information. We also welcome your suggestions; please contact us at: berlitz@apaguide.co.uk
www.insightguides.com/berlitz